LEGENDS, LORE
AND TRUE TALES
OF UTAH

LEGENDS, LORE
AND TRUE TALES
OF UTAH

LYNN ARAVE

THE
History
PRESS

Published by The History Press
Charleston, SC
www.historypress.com

Copyright © 2022 by Lynn Arave
All rights reserved

Front cover, top: Photo by A.J. Russell, public domain; *bottom*: Utah State Historical Society.
Back cover, top: *Salt Lake Telegram*, July 20, 1903; *middle*: Digitized by J. Willard Marriott Library, University of Utah; *bottom*: Utah State Historical Society.

First published 2022

Manufactured in the United States

ISBN 9781467150675

Library of Congress Control Number: 2022935410

To Wayne Wahlquist, my geography professor at Weber State University. Even though I hardly listened in class and never opened the textbook—and received a C grade—when I took his class, way back in the summer of 1976, he instilled in me a love of maps. Closely reading quadrangle maps, I discovered strange and intriguing place-names in Utah. Researching those odd places eventually led to my love of history, too—and this book.

CONTENTS

CONTENTS

ACKNOWLEDGEMENTS

Credit goes to my wife, LeAnn Flygare Arave, for putting up with my endless research and talk about history.

Also, two of my sons, Roger Arave and Taylor Arave, greatly assisted with their technical knowledge and computer skills. In addition, Roger and Taylor provided some photos, as did my daughter, Liz Arave Hafen. My daughter-in-law Whitney Arave also let me use some of her great photographs.

The Utah State Historical Society and Daughters of Utah Pioneers also supplied antique pictures. And newspapers.com was essential in much of the research for this book.

INTRODUCTION

The material for this book was primarily obtained via newspaper research by the author. Thousands of hours were spent scouring old Utah newspapers by keywords to find aspects of Utah history not found in standard history books. Some unexpected gems were found accidentally during those long searches.

Many "what ifs?" were found. These are things that could have made Utah's history slightly different or, sometimes, substantially changed forever.

A number of the chapters herein derive from exhaustive research conducted while the author was employed as a full-time reporter/editor with the *Deseret News*.

Most of the information stems from the vast curiosity of the author—who, what, when, where, why and how?

Some of the chapters were previously published in the *Deseret News* and the *Ogden Standard-Examiner*. With newspaper resources dwindling and readership at an all-time low, these fascinating historical pieces are published here together.

Other content is from the author's Google blog, *Mystery of Utah History*, where history buffs can read even more obscure Utah history.

This book is also a sequel, of sorts, to one of the author's previous books from The History Press (cowritten by Ray Boren), *Detour Utah: Mysteries, Legends and Peculiar Places*.

Note that this book does not delve into the realm of ghosts in Utah. That subject has been well covered in other books.

PART I

WHAT'S IN A NAME?

1

UTAH NAME DUPLICATION ABOUNDS

It is surprising how many geographical place-names are duplicated in the state of Utah. Unique names are a rarity, and duplication abounds.

You would think that Weber County settlers would not have named two canyons Coldwater Canyon, but they did—even though they are only about six air miles apart.

In Salt Lake County, it is even worse. There are three different Twin Peaks in twenty miles of the Wasatch Mountains, stretching from above the University of Utah to just south of the Snowbird ski resort. And statewide, there are another twelve Twin Peaks to be found.

However, Carbon County is the granddaddy of duplicates, with six different Bear Canyons. And if you ever become lost in Utah's outdoors, hope it is not in a Dry Canyon. There are some forty-six canyons in the Beehive State sharing that title. Rescuers could easily become confused.

The nation's second-driest state has a fleet of Dry Canyons. Tooele County alone contains five Dry Canyons. Kane and Duchesne Counties have four each. Of Utah's twenty-nine counties, only five lack a Dry Canyon. There are Dry Canyons northeast of Brigham City, another by the North Ogden Divide, one in Ogden Canyon, one east of the town of Uintah and one in Morgan County.

"Dry" is also one of the more popular geographical monikers in Utah. There are some 250 "Dry" names, counting canyons, hollows, forks, creeks, lakes and washes.

Coldwater Canyon in North Ogden is the second such named canyon in Weber County, as name repetition abounds in Utah. *Author photo.*

The second-most-popular name is "Cottonwood," with forty different versions. Grand and San Juan Counties each boast four different Cottonwood Canyons. "Pole" is the third most popular, with thirty-eight variations. Utah County has four Pole Canyons.

To round out the ten most common Utah canyon place-names, there are thirty separate Rock Canyons, thirty Spring Canyons, twenty-nine Water Canyons, twenty-nine Trail Canyons, twenty-six Bear Canyons, twenty-two Long Canyons and twenty Horse Canyons.

Big, Black, Box Elder, Broad, Bull, Coal, Corral, Cow, Coyote, Deep, Fish, Flat, Maple, Mill, Pine, Red and Sawmill are monikers for ten or more Utah canyons.

Besides canyons, there are at least two dozen different Narrows in Utah, including the world-famous Zion Narrows. In addition, there are sixteen different Black Mountains to hike in Utah, fourteen Little Mountains and eleven Bald Mountains.

Other heavily used Utah monikers include Mud Springs (fifty versions), Willow Springs (forty), Cottonwood Springs (twenty-six), Rock Springs (twenty-six) and Cold Springs (twenty-one). Little Valley is the most-used valley term, with twenty-nine versions, including a Little Valley that's above South Farmington. Birch Creek has thirty-two renditions, Willow Creek has twenty-six and Cottonwood Creek has twenty-four.

There are more than two dozen Spring Hollows and Dry Forks in Utah. There are more places named Left-Hand and Right-Hand than anyone would want.

Lake names are not unique, either. There are fifteen Blue Lakes, fifteen Dry Lakes, thirteen Mud Lakes, seven Big Lakes and four separate Bear Lakes in the Beehive State.

The High Uintas contains many duplicate names. For example, there are at least two Lost Lakes, a pair of Wall Lakes, several Island Lakes and two Lilly Lakes.

To be fair, Utah does contain some unique and colorful place-names. Among them are the following: Accident Canyon, Ant Peak, Baboon Seep, Bellyache Canyon, Beer Bottle Spring, Blubber Creek, Brew Canyon, Convulsion Canyon, Dead Ox Peak, Girl Hollow, Hang Dog Creek, Horsethief Canyon, Keg Spring, Noah's Ark, No Man's Canyon, No Man's Mountain, Shoofly Hill, Skull Crack Canyon, Sunday Canyon and Weed Basin.

Finally, Hell Canyon in Morgan County is not an unusual title, but it does connect directly with Paradise Canyon.

2

UTAH'S FISHIEST TALE

SARDINE CANYON

Thousands of people a day motor along at fifty-five miles per hour—or more—on the four-lane Highway 89/91 through what is almost always referred to today as Sardine Canyon, the main passageway between Brigham City and Cache Valley/Logan. How that fishy moniker has been affixed to a mountainous area devoid of any truly narrow geography or fishing areas begs an investigation.

It's especially curious, as today's highway does not even travel through the original Sardine Canyon of pioneer times. So, first, a geographical sketch of the area is in order.

Although place-names can eventually become what the general populace keeps calling a location, today's Sardine Canyon is not the original of pioneer times.

Technically speaking, Highway 89/91, an approximately eighteen-mile stretch from Box Elder to Cache County, traverses three separate canyons, none of them named Sardine by official U.S. Geological Survey designation or State of Utah highway maps.

The highway departs Brigham City and travels east and north through Box Elder Canyon to the community of Mantua. Traveling steeply uphill, the highway next encounters Dry Canyon, which ends at Sardine Summit (elevation 5,899 feet). After the road takes a steep downhill segment to Dry Lake, Wellsville Canyon completes the trilogy of canyons into Cache Valley.

It is today's populace and news media that favor calling all three sites Sardine Canyon that overshadows any geography lesson or official maps.

Looking south to Sardine Summit in Sardine Canyon. Note the original Sardine Canyon Highway on the round hill on the left. *Author photo.*

The road alignment through the area has changed significantly over the decades. The first Mormon settlers on the way to Cache County in the fall of 1856 likely traveled about the same route to Sardine Summit and to about Dry Lake as we do today. However, those travelers then—presumably because of water sources and a more gradual route—headed directly east to Sardine Spring. They then followed the original Sardine Canyon northeast into Cache Valley and near today's Hyrum Reservoir and Mount Sterling Cemetery. That was the original path into the valley.

The first real road in the area went through the side canyon that begins just north of Sardine Summit, following part of the original pioneer route, but it then headed east along today's Mount Pisgah Road and into McMurdle Hollow, then into the community of Hyrum.

The first newspaper mention of the name Sardine Canyon that could be located is from Logan in the fall of 1880. A map from September 4, 1878, in the Cache County Surveyor's Office also uses the name. (In 1878, there was a side route possible through Wellsville Canyon instead of Sardine, but that was considered a secondary route at the time.)

A 1915 newspaper article described the experience of driving a Studebaker "Light Six" model through the northern section of the route south into Box Elder County. Mr. L.E. Dresbach drove the automobile, loaded with five people. It was previously "regarded as impossible" to make such a trip in a car. "To Paradise and then west over the Sardine Canyon road practically in high gear and at the rate of 25 miles per hour until the top of the cutoff was reached," it was reported in the newspaper.

A steam shovel cuts a new, more direct road between Brigham City and Cache County in the fall of 1926. The $5,000 project was designed to eliminate some of the sharp curves in the mountain road between Mantua and Wellsville. This work represented a string of different routes, all in the so-called Sardine Canyon area that is busy Highway 89 today. *Courtesy of Utah State Historical Society.*

In the 1920s, the next version of road started about one thousand feet north of the original pioneer route. This road wound around the ridge east of Dry Lake. It is still visible while driving along US 89/91 today. The road, the first alignment to be paved through the area, eventually intersected the original Sardine Canyon. Portions of this road are still paved, but weather is eroding the asphalt, and sections have been removed.

According to newspaper reports, the second version of the route to Cache Valley opened in September 1924, was twenty-four feet wide and had a maximum grade of 6 percent. It cost $200,000 to construct this nine-mile section of road between Mantua and Wellsville.

This road was also a landmark for the west, marking the completion of the last link of a highway from Grand Canyon National Park to Zion National Park and north to Yellowstone National Park.

Furthermore, the road with its compact dirt composition and lower grades was open in winter much more often than was the original highway through the area. This meant that Cache Valley was isolated not for months during the snow season, but more like weeks. "Hundreds of 'autoists' who already traveled over the new road are high in their praise" of the new gravel/hard dirt road, the newspaper reported.

By the following month, the county believed it had solved the snow blockage problem in Sardine Canyon by constructing a special cabin for a winter patrolman, who would live there in the winter and have a "two-ton tractor" to plow the snow.

Despite all the initial praise for the second "Sardine" alignment, there were serious travel problems in later years. For example, in January 1949, this road was closed for a full month. The winter of 1948–49 was northern Utah's snowiest and coldest winter season on record. (Even today's modern Sardine Canyon route can be plagued by snow and ice. In fact, Sardine Canyon often makes the news because of periodic winter accidents reported there.)

The third and final alignment is today's road, built in the 1950s and opened in 1960. It was constructed in part because of the shortcomings that the previous road's closures experienced in the winter of 1949. It traverses down from Sardine Summit on a straight shot to Dry Lake and offers a much shorter and smoother route to Cache Valley than its two predecessors, exiting the canyon into Wellsville.

By the early twenty-first century, this highway had been widened from two lanes to four.

Having established the three variations in the roads through the area, the examination can now return to the original query of Sardine Canyon's name and its three possible origins.

Sardine Summit in Sardine Canyon, with the Wellsville Mountains in the background. *Author photo.*

IN THE FALL OF 1856, the first settlers on the way to Cache Valley stopped near a spring one and a half miles east of what is now known as Dry Lake. It is here that one of the legends claims that these pioneers ate a sardine-can lunch, hence the name of the greater area many decades later. Some variations of this legend claim that these settlers left the sardine can or cans by the trail near Sardine Spring. Later travelers spotted them, and the name was born. However, did cans of sardines exist in 1856? Could the travelers have gone west?

"I think it's possible," the webmaster of www.sardineking.com, out of California, said of cans of sardines existing in Utah in 1856. "I can't think of why a settler would not have wanted to bring a case of sardines with them if they were traveling by horse and wagon. Canned sardines keep very well."

Furthermore, it was indicated that while tin cans were around in 1856, sardines were not canned in the United States until after that. They would have had to have come from Europe and would thus be rarer than a few decades later. (Also, what if the pioneers had eaten a different sort of lunch in the area? How does "Tuna Canyon" or "Steak Canyon" sound?)

Still, the railroad didn't reach Utah until fourteen years later, in 1869. So all of the Mormon pioneers prior to the iron horse had to walk or take a horse, wagon or handcart some 1,300 miles to Salt Lake City. Thus, if a pioneer possessed one or more cans of sardines and brought them along, would they have kept them unopened and uneaten for all of that distance and for weeks or months after, before a future 80-plus-mile trek from Salt Lake to the Cache Valley? They might have saved them in reserve or as a delicacy for as long as possible, though it seems that after several hard winters during the Mormon pioneers' early years, all the canned sardines would have been used up.

SECOND, DID THE FIRST pioneer settlers headed for Cache County believe one of the canyons in the area between Brigham City and Logan was particularly tight or narrow, leading to the name?

The alignment of today's US 89/91 offers no unusually narrow sections. That's why many have pondered the origin of the sardine name, given the lack of geological support. The original Sardine Canyon is narrower than today's version, but it does not appear "sardine" narrow.

An circa 1910 photograph of the original Sardine Canyon is housed in the online archives of Utah State University. This picture shows the stream dominating the canyon at the time, though the canyon itself is not particularly narrow, lacking steep walls.

THIRD, DID THE PRESENCE of tiny, sardine-like fish spotted in a stream along the original Sardine Canyon inspire the canyon's name?

Several professors of aquatic ecology at Utah State University lend support to this claim. "I have heard anecdotally that they (Cache Valley's first settlers) saw whitefish (*Prosopium williamsoni*), which could resemble a sardine to the general public and which were likely abundant in these areas (and still are in the Logan River)," Phaedra Budy, professor and aqautic research ecologist in the Department of Ecology Center, Watershed Sciences, at Utah State University, stated.

Charles P. Hawkins, another professor in that department at USU, agrees, especially if the water source is perennial so that it can support naturally occurring fish.

The first pioneers might have passed by as many as three different springs in Sardine Canyon: Sardine Spring, which was the source of year-round water and spawned a stream; the "Pothole Spring" farther east; and Hall Spring, a little farther north. In addition, South Grove Spring is located about 1,200 feet north of Sardine Spring and feeds into Sardine Canyon. And, since at least 1960, there has been a man-made ditch draining Sardine Spring, with some underground piping.

The original Sardine Canyon was homesteaded by James and Margaret Bradshaw in the late 1800s. They had a camp with milk cows and made

Mountain whitefish. *National Park Service photo.*

butter near Sardine Spring. The land was next owned by the Church of Jesus Christ of Latter-day Saints and part of the Wellsville Stake welfare farm grazing area.

So, the first and third legends appear to be the most plausible. Could it be that the pioneer lunch of sardines, their discarded cans along the trail, plus later glimpses of small, sardine-sized fish in streams to the east of today's modern highway, combined to cement the Sardine Canyon name? That's the most likely conclusion.

It should be noted that only one other officially named Sardine Canyon exists in the entire United States. Strangely, it is also in northern Utah, located as a side canyon on the south side of Ogden Canyon, just southeast of today's Alaskan Inn (formerly the site of the Hermitage).

This other Sardine Canyon is approximately thirty air miles from the much more well-known Sardine Canyon. This smaller canyon is extremely narrow. As its beginning is elevated several dozen feet above the nearby Ogden Canyon's paved highway, it is likely often not noticed by travelers. Since no other canyon using the name "sardine" exists in the United States, could these two canyons be connected somehow? After all, what are the odds that both would end up in Utah and be only some thirty air miles apart?

John W. Van Cott, who authored *Utah Place Names*, cross-referenced the origin of the Sardine Peak's name to Sardine Canyon in Cache County. Why he did this is unknown. (Van Cott died in 2006.) Sardine Park (elevation 7,485 feet) connects to the other Sardine Canyon in Weber County. There are two other sardine-nicknamed places in that Weber County area, just north of Snow Basin Resort. "Little Sardine Peak" (elevation 5,970) is often referenced. Also, "Sardine Hill" (elevation 5,461) is nearby. Today, this Weber County "sardine" has its own popularity, with a mountain-bike loop through the area.

It has to be more than a coincidence that both of the sardine-named canyons in the country are located in the state of Utah, just thirty miles apart: the well-known Sardine Canyon, along the well-traveled route of US 89 between Brigham City and Logan; and the little-known Sardine Canyon off of Ogden Canyon, south of the Alaskan Inn and not far from the original historic Hermitage Inn.

The Hermitage opened in August 1905. It boasted twenty-five rooms and cost some $30,000 to build. A second story was soon added with another sixteen rooms. Horse-drawn buggies carried passengers to the resort before a rail line was built in Ogden Canyon. Trout and chicken dinners were the specialty of the rustic Hermitage. Boating was also popular in the area

Hermitage Hotel, 1918. *Public domain*.

Hermitage Hotel, 1910. *Public domain*.

near the hotel. (Two of the owners' own children drowned in a boating accident there.)

The Hermitage had a run of some thirty-four years. An explosion and fire leveled the resort in January 1939, and it was never rebuilt. In fact, the Hermitage received all of its original water from Sardine Canyon, according to the *Ogden Daily Standard* of November 5, 1912.

William "Billy" Wilson, who built the Hermitage out of lumber in the area, also made a dam in Sardine Canyon to supply his business with ample yet independent water, according to the *Standard* of May 17, 1912.

This other Sardine Canyon was also famous for another event. It was the site of the first open-air (non-Mormon) Christian religious services in Utah. According to the *Ogden Daily Standard* of May 30, 1913, Christians from Brigham City to Salt Lake City gathered at the Hermitage and then traveled up the trail to the nearby Sardine Canyon for outdoor services. Today, part of Sardine Canyon, as well as Sardine Peak, are accessed by a mountain-bike trail.

The reason that the two canyons have the same name may remain a mystery. The Ogden Canyon Sardine version is indeed a narrow and small canyon deserving of a sardine-can title. The name of the Highway 89 Sardine Canyon will always remain a little fishy and offbeat.

"DERN!" IT'S HILL AIR FORCE BASE

H ill Air Force Base could have had a different name.

The original Utah proposal was to name the base Dern Field, after Utah's sixth governor, George Henry Dern (served 1925–33). He was later the secretary of war under President Franklin Roosevelt from 1933 until his death in 1936.

According to the *Davis County Clipper* of January 24, 1990, it was U.S. representative J.W. (James William) Robinson, a Democrat from Utah, who made the suggestion to name the base after Dern. This wasn't just to honor the late governor and secretary for his high political offices. According to the *Ogden Standard-Examiner* of February 4, 1940, Dern had "made an inspection" in 1935 of the potential air base land in northern Utah and "became very sympathetic towards its potential possibilities." "Secretary Dern's efforts were responsible in a large measure for renewed interest in this project," the *Standard-Examiner* reported.

This led to the War Department securing options on 4,135 acres of land in the area that the Ogden Chamber of Commerce was promoting as ideal for a future air base and ordnance depot site.

Although most Utahns likely agreed it was a good idea to honor Dern with the base's name, it apparently did not square with U.S. Army Air Force policy. According to the 1990 *Clipper* story, U.S. Army general H.H. Arnold responded to Robinson's naming proposal by saying that the base "would probably be named after an army flier who performed distinguished flying service in Utah, or whose death occurred in that vicinity."

Hangar No. 1 Complex, Hill Field. *Survey number: HAER UT-85-O. Library of Congress.*

Notwithstanding, the *Hill Top Times* of January 1, 1946, stated, "War Department General Order No. 9 names site OAD 'Hill Field' in honor of Major Ployer P. Hill." (Hill Field was the base's original name; it was renamed Hill Air Force Base on February 5, 1948.)

Major Ployer "Pete" Hill was killed while piloting the experimental Boeing B-17 (Model 299) bomber at Wright Field, Ohio, on October 30, 1935. However, Ployer Hill had no ties to Utah at the time, and Wright Field was more than 1,600 miles from today's Hill Air Force Base.

The fact that the sandy area of today's Hill Air Force Base is located on a hill, elevated from much of the surrounding area, has made the title more appropriate over the decades.

There is no indication of displeasure with the base's name, nor is there any known move to rename it. In fact, during its early years, Hill Field paid tribute to the daring test pilot on the anniversary of his death. "Field Recalls Tragic Death of Major Hill. Army Base Pays Tribute to Officer Who Died Seven Years Ago," was an October 29, 1942 headline in the *Standard-Examiner*.

The base's naming finally had its late-arriving Utah connection in the 1960s. The *Standard-Examiner* of November 7, 1965, reported that Major Hill's only son, also named Ployer P. Hill, served a tour at Hill AFB as a major from 1964 to 1966, prior to a combat mission in Vietnam. (The younger Hill died on January 21, 2008, at the age of eighty-three in Florida.)

Yes, Dern Air Force Base doesn't sound right after more than eighty years. It could have been, but the Hill name is both appropriate and deserving. And the descendants of Major Hill are very proud that there is a significant air base with their name.

"Teeming City Thrives on What Was Only Wind-Swept Flat Four Years Ago" was a headline in the *Ogden Standard-Examiner* of February 7, 1943. "Ogden air depot at Hill Field stands as a monument to the ingenuity, industry and determination of the people of Utah," the story stated. Counter to the former wind-swept land, there now exists there "a city comprised of huge repair hangars and shops, humming with activity; great warehouses with hundreds of thousands of air corps supply items; administrative office buildings covering many acres; miles of track over which are shunted hundreds of freight cars every day."

The *Standard*'s description continued: "Like any other modern city, Hill Field has many schools, theatres, a chapel, living quarters consisting of both civilian and military barracks, a fire station, cafeterias, utilities, including gas, water and electrical installations, a well-developed police organization, and its own transportation system.…The physical growth of Hill Field has been prodigious."

Nine months later, another newspaper reported on the same transition of former open land in northern Utah. "One Time Farm Area Now Industrialized," was a headline in the *Salt Lake Tribune* of November 7, 1943. The article continued, "Farmers who used to till the soil on a vast expanse of valley land in northern Davis County never thought more about industrial plants or anything which was a very far cry from agriculture."

"Today they gaze at the $22,000,000 rambling air service command headquarters called Hill Field." The *Tribune* article also stated that thousands of workers now work at the base. (In fact, the area was at one time part of what was called the "Sandridge," a sandy area that was more for dry farming in pioneer times.)

"Hill Field existed as an idea as far back as 1935.…Sheltered by high mountains, far enough inland to minimize chances of enemy attack, easily accessible by rail and not too far from the Pacific coast," the *Tribune* stated.

Hill Field, Airplane Repair Hangars Nos. 1–4. *Survey number: HAER UT-85-O. Library of Congress.*

Hill Field was then the nerve center for twelve sub-depots in eight states, all of which are controlled and supplied by Hill Field. "Only 12 miles from Ogden and 30 miles from Salt Lake City, Hill Field grew up in the midst of what was to become one of the most acute labor shortage areas in the war industrialized west," the story reported.

WHO WAS UTAH'S ST. GEORGE?

Who was Saint George?
Located in the heart of Utah's southwest corner, the city of St. George is one of the fastest-growing communities in the nation. But who is the city named after, and why is "Saint" affixed to this name?

Most historians agree on the origin of the city's name, but there is an alternate version out there.

"St. George itself was named in honor of Elder George A. Smith, an early LDS Church apostle and first counselor to President Brigham Young. Although Smith did not participate in the town's settlement, he personally selected most of the company of the pioneers of 1861," writes Bart C. Anderson in the *Utah History Encyclopedia*.

Anderson states on St. George City's website (www.sgcity.org) that Elder Smith was also nicknamed "the potato saint," because he had encouraged early pioneers to eat raw, unpeeled potatoes to "cure a troublesome bout with scurvy."

Andrew Jenson, an early twentieth-century historian for the Church of Jesus Christ of Latter-day Saints, also believed the town's name came in honor of Elder Smith. "From the very beginning, the location was named St. George in honor of Apostle George A. Smith," Jenson wrote in *Encyclopedia History of the Church of Jesus Christ of Latter-day Saints*, published in 1941.

Jenson said St. George was founded in 1861 by missionaries called in the October General Conference of that year to settle there with their families. By December 1, 1861, they had made a camp a half mile northeast of where the St. George Temple stands today.

St. George is the largest city in southwest Utah and has the state's warmest climate. *Author photo.*

Elder Smith was grandfather to George Albert Smith, the church's eighth president.

John W. Van Cott, who wrote *Utah Place Names* in 1990, also agrees that St. George was named for Elder George A. Smith. He states that the naming came even before settlers arrived and called Smith "Father of the South." "It was half-humorously suggested that if other churches could have Saints, Mormons could, too," Van Cott says at the end of the paragraph regarding the naming of St. George.

In fact, the most historically famous St. George is a figure in early Christianity considered the patron saint of England, according to the *Catholic Encyclopedia*.

Rufos Wood Leigh, who compiled *Five Hundred Utah Place Names* in 1961, also sides with the Smith origin story. Utah historian Milton R. Hunter also says that the town of St. George was named after George A. Smith in his 1940 book *Brigham Young the Colonizer* (page 82).

However, in a different article included on St. George's website, Anderson states that there is an alternative to this St. George origin story. Philip St. George Cooke was a non-Mormon who may have donated a good share of equipment and wagons to Utah's southwest. Anderson describes Cooke as a trusted friend of Brigham Young. Cooke, a U.S. Army officer, also led the Mormon Battalion from New Mexico to California.

Left: George Albert Smith. *By Thomas Hunter, Lith. Philadelphia, Pa. Published by Anderson & Girardet, Salt Lake City, Utah, circa 1875. Public domain.*

Right: Philip St. George Cooke. *Photographer unknown, circa 1876. BYU University Lee Library L. Tom Perry Special Collections; MSS P 16. Public domain.*

St. George is not the only Mormon settlement named after a "saint." There are at least two more. St. David, Arizona, located southeast of Tucson, was named in honor of David Patten Kimball. He was the presiding LDS Church authority in the area from 1881 to 1882.

According to the *Utah History Encyclopedia*, St. Charles, Idaho, located on the northwest side of Bear Lake, was named after Elder Charles C. Rich, a Mormon apostle. He was one of the first early settlers. In 1864, Brigham Young honored Rich by naming Rich County, Utah, and the town of St. Charles after him.

5

WASATCH OR WAHSATCH?
AND MORE

Is it Wasatch or Wahsatch? How about Uinta or Uintah? The answer is, they are all correct, depending on the usage, and all have some interesting history behind them.

Though "Wasatch" is the accepted spelling for the mountain range and a county east of Salt Lake, there once was a town called Wahsatch located along I-80 at the east end of Echo Canyon, about twenty-four miles southwest of Evanston, Wyoming. It was named for Chief Wahsatch, a Shoshone Indian whose name was spelled that way, according to John W. Van Cott in his book *Utah Place Names*.

Wahsatch sprang up as a railroad town in 1868. Hundreds lived there in its frantic heyday, but eventually it became desolate when Evanston took over as the area's railroad hub. Now a ghost town, it is still listed as Wahsatch on the official Utah highway map. It is apparently one of the few instances in Utah in which the name is still spelled with an extra *h*.

Kent Powell, a Utah State Historical Society historian, said he's also wondered if Wasatch and Wahsatch weren't just two different spellings of the same word. Chief Wahsatch, he said, likely did not learn to spell his name in English, so someone else probably came up with the spelling.

Clarence King of the U.S. Geological Survey worked in Utah in 1869. His photograph *Wahsatch Limestone Cliffs* supports the notion of that spelling once being applied to the mountain range. *Wasatch* is a Ute Indian word meaning "mountain pass" or "low place in a high mountain," according to Van Cott.

It is not a misspelling on this road sign. It is a variation of "Wasatch," found near the Wyoming border in northeast Utah. *Author photo.*

Besides the lone place-name using the "Wahsatch" spelling, a few current organizations and events have adopted it. For example, there's the Wahsatch Shooters Association and two footraces, the Wahsatch Steeplechase and the Wahsatch Rendezvous.

There is another Utah place-name spelled with and without an extra *h*: Uintah and Uinta. There seems to be some question, even a little controversy, about the missing or added letter. According to History to Go, an online historical resource of the Utah State Historical Society/Utah State History Department, early maps usually attached an *h* to the end of Uintah. However, it was left off of Major John Wesley Powell's publications from his 1869 geographic expedition as being unnecessary for pronunciation of the word.

There's even a possible dark side to the Uintah spelling. Some descendants of the original Native Americans of the Uintah Valley Reservation suspect that in 1902 the federal government added the *h* to distort the true identity of the Uinta Indians and to distance itself from an 1861 executive order that created the Uinta Valley River Reservation. At the same time, they wondered if it could have simply been a mistake by a government typist.

Uinta/Uintah also is a Ute Indian word, and there is some disagreement about its meaning. It either refers to land at the edge of pines or streams of water, or living high up where timber grows, according to *A History of Uintah County* by Doris Karren Burton.

Local historians see the spelling more as a matter of expediency. "I have been told that for Uinta/Uintah that Uinta is applied to natural features—Uinta Basin, Uinta Mountains, Uinta River—while Uintah is for political names—Uintah County, Uintah Indian Reservation, Uintah Stake, etc.," Kent Powell said.

Burton essentially agrees. "The National Board of Geographic Names applies the spelling Uintah to political subdivisions, such as counties, reservations, etc., and the spelling Uinta to mountains, streams, and other geographic features." For example, there's Uintah County, the town of

Uinta C (Eocene) exposed in the Uintah Basin. *Photo by Kenneth Carpenter (CC BY-SA 4.0).*

Uintah in Weber County and Uintah High School in Vernal. And there is the Uinta Mountains and the Uinta National Forest.

Floyd O'Neil, director emeritus of the American West Center at the University of Utah, says there's really no way to know for certain how the spellings came to be, adding, "This all creates a great spelling bog."

LAYTON'S ODDLY TITLED GENTILE STREET

Perhaps no other street name in Davis County's largest city is more unusual than Gentile Street. This street with the striking moniker spans the west to the east, more than nine miles in length. Most residents probably rarely give the name a second thought. Some erroneously pronounce it "Gen-till."

According to Layton City's website (www.laytoncity.org) and the Utah State History site (history.utah.gov), the city's territory was settled in 1851 by early members of the Church of Jesus Christ of Latter-day Saints. The settlers were grouped around the natural streams in the area (Kays Creek and Holmes Creek), as water was scarce, until canals were created. By 1877, the Davis and Weber Canal had been dug, opening new areas of settlement. By 1882, Gentile Street (west of today's Main Street) was open for travel.

The street's name came from the only two resident families on the east end of the road who were not members of the LDS Church. Giles Bowler and Joseph Hudson lived along the road on the city's west side and referred to themselves as "Gentiles." The street name was born. (One Layton historian, Bill Sanders, former Layton Heritage Museum director, suspected that those families may have actually just been less active or former Mormon Church members, not true Gentiles.)

To Jews, Gentiles are anyone who is not Jewish. For LDS (Mormon) Church members, the term *Gentile* refers to anyone who is not Mormon, according to the *American Heritage Dictionary of the English Language*.

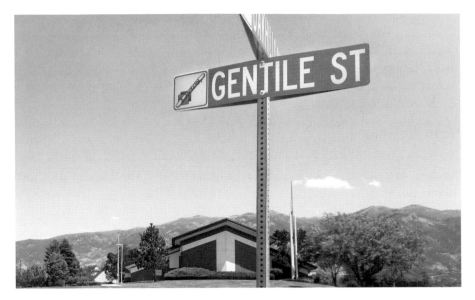

Gentile Street is one of the main roads in Layton City and boasts a colorful but uncertain history. *Author photo*.

Later, a Protestant church was once located along Gentile Street, further solidifying that name.

The only other theory for the name comes from the late Bob Waite of Kaysville, who majored in history at Weber State University. He said that the old immigrant trail that traversed the western portion of Davis County had a supply station near the western end of today's Gentile Street. It was manned by "Gentiles" and so could have led to the street's name.

Ironically, in the twenty-first century, there are three different LDS Chapels located along Gentile Street, two on the east side and one on the west. There is also a Kingdom Hall of the Jehovah's Witnesses on the east section of Gentile Street.

Gentile Street also extends westward, beyond Layton. Even though some Syracuse City street signs call it 3700 West Street, some official signs there list the road as Gentile Street.

Also of interest is that at least one of the historic homes on the East Gentile half of the street sports address numbers that denote when the home was built, such as 1877, rather than an exact geographical reference point.

The area not far from today's Layton City Hall was originally referred to as Scotland, because that's where its earliest settlers came from.

Today's Fort Lane road name comes from Little Fort Lane, its name in the nineteenth century, when a fort was built in that area to protect residents from Native Americans.

Layton also has a Chapel Street, home to an LDS Chapel as well as a Catholic church.

The idea of naming a place after non-Mormons is not unique to Layton. The Gem Valley in Grace, Idaho, and the surrounding area was originally named Gentile Valley, in 1870, likely before Layton's Gentile Street was named. The name derives from the non-Mormons who settled that southeast Idaho valley.

BRYCE CANYON AND
ZION NAME CHANGES

Bryce Canyon wasn't always accepted as the name to a scenic and colorful rocky wonderland in southern Utah. In 1920—even before Bryce was a national monument—there was a strong movement to rename the area something different to better conform to geology and geography.

"New Name Wanted for Bryce Canyon," was a June 8, 1920 headline in the *Salt Lake Herald*. A statewide contest was held by the Utah State Automobile Association to find a more suitable title for Bryce, as it wasn't really a canyon but an amphitheater.

At that time, the early twentieth century, Bryce was also sometimes referred to as Temple of the Gods. That is how the place was labeled on official federal maps. Others referred to it as Bryce's Canyon. Since Colorado boasted a place named Garden of the Gods, the name Temple of the Gods was considered confusing and not suitable.

The winner of the contest to rename Bryce would earn an all-expenses-paid trip to Bryce and Zion National Park. "Bryce Canyon to Be Renamed" read a June 8, 1920 headline in the *Ogden Standard-Examiner*. All major Utah papers carried news of the big contest.

Apparently, many early visitors had been complaining that Bryce Canyon was not an accurate title for the scenic marvel and that a new title was needed before the site gained worldwide fame in ensuing years.

Bryce Canyon was named for Ebenezer Bryce, a Mormon pioneer who homesteaded in the area in 1874. He also reportedly proclaimed it was a "helluva place to lose a cow."

Bryce Canyon was almost renamed in 1920 because it was not geologically a canyon. *Author photo.*

Big Bend in Zion National Park was originally titled Raspberry Bend, as some of the park's early names changed. *Author photo.*

Bryce became a national monument in 1923 and a national park in 1928. The renaming contest, however, did not go smoothly. "Garfield County Protests Renaming of Bryce Canyon," stated a June 12, 1920 headline in the *Salt Lake Herald*. That story reported that the Utah State Automobile Association agreed that Garfield County, home to Bryce Canyon, should have a strong say in the renaming process but that the contest would continue. "We are not trying to dictate the name of anything and we would not attempt to foist an undesirable name upon any section of the state," W.D. Rishel, manager of the association, stated in the *Herald* story.

He continued, "Our efforts in securing a more suitable title were solicited by hundreds of visitors, who declared that Utah is hiding the most singular scenic attraction in the world under the most commonplace title."

When the renaming contest had run its course a few weeks later, it was concluded that the judges could not find a more suitable title, despite hundreds of suggestions by the public. "Bryce Name to Stand" the *Salt Lake Herald* declared on July 8, 1920. "No better title than the present name of Bryce Canyon was found by the board of judges," the story concluded.

Jump forward eight years, to 1927, and the leading new name for Bryce Canyon National Park was Utah National Park. The *Ogden Standard-Examiner*

The Great White Throne was originally known as El Gobernadore. This view is from atop Angels Landing. *Roger Arave photo.*

of July 21, 1927, states that Governor George H. Dern said that the Utah National Park name was "highly objectionable," because "much money had been expended in bringing the name of Bryce to the attention of travelers."

Here's a look at some of the natural feature names that have changed at nearby Zion National Park since its days of the pioneers.

Raspberry Bend was the original name for the "Big Bend" in Zion Canyon. El Gobernadore was the earliest of titles for the Great White Throne. Wylie Camp was the name of the first public camping place in Zion. This was essentially a tent camping resort and is approximately located where the Zion Lodge is today. The name for the Three Patriarchs has been modified over the decades. Today, the Court of the Patriarchs in the most common title for the area.

The desert varnish of colors in the rock walls of Zion were originally labeled the Streaked Wall and the Brown Wall. The Streaked Wall was on the west side of the canyon; the Brown Wall was on the east. These were located between today's Zion Lodge on the north and the East and West Temples on the south.

FORSAKEN TITLE

WATKINS DAM

Would you like to go fishing or boating at northern Utah's Watkins Dam?

Where's that? What?

Sometimes, popular usage over time can supersede official titles.

We're talking Willard Bay here, but its original name was Arthur V. Watkins Dam, or Watkins Bay.

The nearby town of Willard and/or Willard Peak soon became the water reservoir's official namesake by popular reference. (In fact, one of the few places you will find the Watkins name used today is on the U.S. Bureau of Reclamation's official website.)

Willard Bay, located eleven miles northwest of Ogden and adjacent to the Great Salt Lake, is often taken for granted. But this artificial treasure has a history worth examining. It is surprising how little of it is in the history books or accessible via Google. Thanks to some additional information supplied by the Weber Basin Water Conservancy District, here's the scoop on "Willard Bay."

This water project was authorized by an act of Congress on August 29, 1949. It was U.S. senator Arthur V. Watkins (R-Utah) who worked to create funding for this project. It became a 14.5-mile-long, roughly rectangle-shaped dike structure that impounds surplus freshwater from reaching the Great Salt Lake. Some seventeen million cubic yards of material were used to create the dam.

The earthen material used in the project is highly compressible. So, in order to allow maximum time for settlement, the dam was constructed in three stages

Arthur V. Watkins Dam or Watkins Bay were the original names for Willard Bay. This view is from Willard Peak. *Liz Arave Hafen photo*.

over a period of more than seven years. The dam was built by the Bureau of Reclamation and completed in 1964. Essentially, a dike was created. The salt water was drained out, and freshwater was then stored inside.

In 1990, a fourth stage of construction entailed restoring the dike crest to its original 4,235 feet above sea level (about 36 feet high), following even more additional but anticipated settlement of the foundation.

Surplus water from the Weber River and its tributaries, which cannot be controlled by mountain reservoirs, as well as winter releases through Gateway and Wanship Power Plants and other private utilities, normally would flow into the Great Salt Lake.

This surplus water is diverted from the Weber River at the Slaterville Diversion Dam, located west of Ogden, and carried north eight miles by the Willard Canal into Willard Bay Reservoir. To meet project needs, water can be returned in the summer from Willard Bay Reservoir to the Weber River and into the Layton Pumping Plant intake channel as needed for irrigation of lands lying along the shores of the Great Salt Lake.

About five miles north along the diversion canal a turnout can also divert water into the Plain City Canal, a privately owned irrigation system. Water can also be released to the Harold Crane Wildlife Management Area and to

Great Salt Lake Minerals through a siphon outlet at the southwest corner of the Willard Bay dike.

Willard Bay Reservoir is the lowest reservoir of the Weber River system. It averages 19 feet in depth and reaches as much as 36 feet. It can hold a maximum of 215,120 acre feet of water (almost twice that of Pineview). Among the Bureau of Reclamation's twenty-five dams in Utah, only Flaming Gorge and Jordanelle reservoirs can hold more water. Operation and maintenance of the dam were turned over to the Weber Basin Water Conservancy District in 1968.

Creating Willard Bay meant the loss of some farmland dating back to the pioneer era. Unlike most area settlements, Willard (originally known as Willow Creek) had most of its farmland on its fringes rather than in its interior. But Willard Bay's creation eventually led to a multiplication of new farmland in northern Utah, thanks to the additional water available.

Principal agriculture products that are sustained or aided by its irrigation water are fruit, vegetables, potatoes, alfalfa, grain and livestock.

Willard Bay State Park came along in 1966. The Utah Division of Parks and Recreation maintains facilities at the site for picnicking. Willard Bay Reservoir is used for camping, picnicking, swimming, boating and water-skiing. Fishing is also available for wipers, walleye, channel catfish, black crappie, smallmouth bass, bluegill, common carp, largemouth bass and

Willard Bay State Park. *Photo by JF Hobbs / CC BY 3.0, via Wikimedia Commons.*

yellow perch. The view of the rocky spires on the mountainside above Willard Bay is simply incredible.

Willard Bay is at its most stunning, though, from the view atop Willard Peak. Its blueness contrasts sharply with the surrounding briny waters of the Great Salt Lake.

Over the decades, there have been proposals to dike off other areas of the east side of the Great Salt Lake and divert surplus water into similar freshwater reservoirs. None have happened, so Willard Bay remains Utah's lone Great Salt Lake side reservoir.

Recently, funding for a feasibility study to see if Willard Bay itself could be further expanded failed to gain approval.

WHY THE PRESIDENTIAL FLAIR FOR OGDEN'S STREETS?

Some of the major streets in Ogden, Utah, have a presidential flair. However, it wasn't always so.

Seventeen of Ogden's main north–south streets are named after U.S. presidents. Knowing the presidents—and their order—can help you find your way around town.

We're talking Washington Boulevard as the city's center thoroughfare. Going east, the full-block streets advance in order to that named after the fifteenth president, James Buchanan. Drop back down to west of Washington Boulevard, and there are two more presidential streets, Lincoln and Grant.

"We have had people comment about our streets being named after the presidents, and generally people think that's kind of cool," Ogden mayor Matthew Godfrey said in 2007. "I'm not sure how much it helps people find their place around, because that requires a knowledge of the presidents in their order, and I don't know of many that have that ability. I think it has worked in the reverse for many of us that live here. The street names help us learn who the presidents were in order."

Juanita Taylor, a lifelong resident of Ogden, lives on her namesake street, Taylor Avenue. "I recall memorizing the presidents when I was young," she said. "That's stuck with me." She said it still helps her find her way around town. It also occasionally applies to her grown children, who also learned the names. But she's not so sure recent generations know anything of the legacy of Ogden's streets, as she did when she was in school.

Left: Fred J. Kiesel (1889–1890). *Utah State Archives, public domain.*

Right: Franklin D. Richards, circa 1862. *C.R. Savage collection at the L. Tom Perry Special Collections, Harold B. Lee Library, Brigham Young University, call number MSS P 24 Item 122.*

Ogden isn't alone in presidential street-naming. Other U.S. cities also use this method, including Kennewick, Washington; Hollywood, Florida; Trenton, New Jersey; and Alcoa, Tennessee. But it's a rarity in Utah.

Noticeably missing from Ogden's streets is a Johnson Avenue, for the seventeen president, Andrew Johnson. Why he's absent is not made clear in the history books. Perhaps it is because Johnson was appointed, not elected, president, and/or because he was impeached. The naming of presidents for Ogden's streets has not continued beyond Grant.

Ogden's presidential streets weren't always named after these American leaders. Originally, some of Ogden's north–south streets were named for prominent leaders of the Church of Jesus Christ of Latter-day Saints. Mormon pioneers settled Ogden; as in Salt Lake City, LDS names dominated. For example, Washington Boulevard was originally Main Street; Lincoln Street was Franklin Street, for Franklin D. Richards; and Grant Avenue was Young Street, for Brigham Young. Also, Jefferson Avenue used to be Smith Street, for Joseph Smith, the founder of the LDS Church.

Why did the name changes happen? It was an attempt to "Americanize" Ogden, according to *A History of Weber County* by Richard C. Roberts and Richard W. Sadler. The first non-Mormon mayor, Fred J. Kiesel (1889–

91), convinced the city council to rename Ogden's streets at a meeting on April 5, 1889.

The focal point was likely the rivalry between the Mormons and non-Mormons in Ogden at the time. The city was experiencing a bigger power struggle than what was happening in Salt Lake City, due to its "Junction City" status as a railroad hub that attracted many more non-Mormons to the area.

However, even some non-LDS-oriented names were changed. Spring Street, Pearl Street and Greer Street also vanished and were replaced with presidential titles.

The only north–south street name left intact was Wall Avenue. It was named for the wall of an 1855 pioneer fort that existed there and extended east to today's Madison Avenue and went from today's Twenty-First to Twenty-Eighth Streets. The wall was eight feet high and cost $40,000. It was never completed.

In later years, the city added streets named for Pierce and Buchanan as the city's roads extended to the foothills.

Kiesel also got the city council to allow for more city growth and to renumber the east–west configuration at the same time. Before 1889, First Street ran along the north side of the LDS Tabernacle block, and Second Avenue was on the south. These boundaries were greatly extended, and the original First Street became Twenty-First Street.

Kiesel cared about roads, though, and set up a poll tax that required all men aged twenty to fifty to work one day a year on the streets or else pay a three-dollar fee.

He also started Ogden's first uniform house numbering system and required all builders in town to have permits. He was keen on a separation of church and state and got a law approved that made it illegal for any city residents to use a church meetinghouse as a school building.

Ogden's Grant Avenue and Twenty-Fourth Street were originally essentially bogs. In the mid-1880s, loads of gravel were brought in to improve Ogden's streets.

The city's first concrete sidewalks came in 1889. The first Ogden street paved was Twenty-Fifth Street from Washington to Wall in 1893 at a cost of $100,000.

FROGWATER OR ARTESIAN WELL IN NORTH OGDEN?

Is it "frogwater" or just artesian well water pouring out of a "stump" in northern Utah?

A historic artesian well flows with history at the top of Washington Boulevard in North Ogden, Utah. East of Lee's Marketplace and north of a McDonald's restaurant at 2650 North Street, water is constantly flowing out of a "tree" stump, thanks to a restoration project in 1999–2000 by the city council and a local Eagle Scout.

Clarence Barker drilled the artesian well in 1930 for irrigation water. Then, in the summer of 1931, the "Stump" came along. Joe Ballif, who had a hamburger stand near the well at 2620 North 390 East and who was already using some of the water for his business, decided to capitalize on the refreshing liquid.

Ballif obtained a cottonwood tree stump from Frank Campbell's front yard at 2594 North 400 East (where a bank is now) to spruce up the well. However, this was the remains of not just any tree. It was what was left of the original and lone tree standing in the area when pioneers arrived in North Ogden in the 1850s. The upper part of the tree had been destroyed by lightning, and Ballif salvaged the stump. It took four horses to haul it to the well a short distance away.

Dewey Lakey, a traveling craftsman, was called in. He cut and chiseled the stump so it could contain a fountain and a yellow light bulb. The water began flowing through the stump. A nearby sign stated, "Good water, isn't it? Try our hamburgers," as an advertisement for Ballif's food outlet.

The artesian well in North Ogden flows out of a replica tree stump, reminiscent of what was in place there from 1931 to about the 1960s. *Author photo*.

In later years, the tree stump deteriorated and much of it rotted away. Ballif's stand went out of business. A steel ring and concrete were added, probably in the 1960s, to shore up the stump, though this meant it lost its treelike appearance.

The well had developed the strange nickname Frogwater by the 1950s. According to Charles "Chick" Hislop, former Weber State University track and cross-country coach, that name took hold in the mid-1950s, when there was an actual tree stump from which the artesian well water emerged. Hislop said he and college kids often frequented the well. Back then, swampland occupied the area, and there were as a lot of noisy frogs around. Hislop recalled in an interview in 2017 the well's nickname. Most people enjoyed the mineral taste of the water, but one college girl didn't and said, "I'm not drinking that frogwater." The name took hold.

The well was a landmark throughout Weber County. In fact, Coach Chick Hislop started having his athletes run to the fountain, exactly ten miles from WSU, beginning in about 1969, for some of their "overdistance" training sessions. The runners could always count on having a refreshing drink of water at the run's end.

Hislop said that, by then, the stump had rotted away and there was cement around the fountain.

He had also directed his prep runners to run to the fountain in the mid-1960s when he was a coach at Ben Lomond High School. That distance was five miles from school to fountain.

The establishment of Acres Market (forerunner to today's grocery store there) in 1999 meant the fountain would be removed. Marc M. Sutherland decided to create a plaque describing the well's history as his Eagle Scout project. With historical interest stirred, the North Ogden City Council became involved and had a ten-foot-high fiberglass replica of the tree stump made and placed near the original well. It was dedicated on May 20, 2000, in a special ceremony attended by some two hundred people.

Now the new "Stump" boasts two drinking fountains on its south side and a large flowing pipe on its north face. Gallon bottles can be filled up in seconds. "It's better than tap water," North Ogden resident Mike Barrow told the *Deseret News* in the summer of 2000 as he filled up more than a dozen jugs with the water. "My whole family drinks it. I guess I should bring some larger jugs." He said the water has been tested for quality and is better than the city of North Ogden's culinary water.

Thirsty kids on bikes and skateboards regularly stop at the fountain for drinks. State senator Robert Montgomery (R-North Ogden) recalled at the

Salt Lake City boasts its own longtime artesian well, located at the southwest corner of 800 South Street and 500 East Street. *Author photo.*

fountain's dedication stopping there frequently as a child for a cold drink. Area residents regularly fill up jugs of the free water.

There's a nearby Veteran's Park, benches and a mini-park in the area today. North Ogden City even has a Christmas Santa house on the site. It is likely that some who pass by never notice the strange-looking well.

Salt Lake City has its own artesian well counterpart to this, located at the southwest corner of 800 South and 500 East. The water flows 24/7 and is free. You just drive up on the south side of 800 South heading east, park, get out and fill up your containers. Well water trickles down from a decorative arch. This well also has a long history.

FROM BLOOMERS AND CHAPS TO DELICATE ARCH

Many take the name of the world-renowned Delicate Arch in Arches National Park for granted. This is no ordinary arch. It has become the symbol not only for Arches National Park (home to more than two thousand stone arches) but also for the entire state of Utah at times.

The first time the name Delicate Arch was used in print was in the *Times Independent* on January 8, 1934. The author was Frank Beckwith, an archaeologist with Arches National Monument. He stated, "This is by far the most delicately chiseled arch in the entire area."

The *Times* provided the following subhead for the section for this statement: "A Beautiful Delicate Arch." It is likely that from that time the name blossomed and was soon the official title of the natural feature.

This park icon was originally called "Bloomer's" or the "Chaps" by area cowboys. Another variation was "Schoolmarm's Bloomers."

The trail to Delicate Arch used to be an ordeal, requiring the use of ladders and handrails. A *Times Independent* report from May 25, 1950, explained that it took some local Girl Scouts half a day to reach Delicate Arch via that original path. On returning to Wolf Ranch, the girls were tired and sunburned. It wasn't until the spring of 1953 that the trail was reworked to its present configuration. This new trail followed a seam in the rocks.

Long before Arches National Park came along, this area north of Moab, Utah, was a huge cattle-ranching site. Early settlers were simply not impressed with scenery when they had to make a living in harsh desert territory.

Delicate Arch was originally named differently by cowboys in the early pioneer days. The first trail to it was much more difficult than today's path. *Author photo.*

The Wolf Ranch, just west of Delicate Arch and near the trailhead to the famous arch, was the most famous of these cattle ranches. It came along in 1898 and was about 150 acres in size, operated by Civil War veteran John Wesley Wolf. According to the *Times Independent* of August 3, 1967, a flood in the Salt Wash of Arches in 1906 washed Wolf's first cabin away, and he had to build another away from the main drainage.

After Wolf sold out and left, sheep were grazed in the area. Also, horses ran free in the region.

The Arches area was completely closed at times in the early 1960s. "Vandalism in Arches Forces Action," was a May 3, 1962 headline in the *Moab Times Independent*. "A two-month siege of destructive vandalism in the Arches National Monument confines has forced park officials to chain the entrance of the scenic attraction and ban visitors from the area from 8 p.m. to 7 a.m.," the newspaper reported. Among the acts of vandalism prompting the action were the destruction of signs, toilets filled with rocks, extreme littering and damage to a footbridge. The closure didn't last long. The place was designated a U.S. National Park in 1971. By then, vandalism had eased up.

Delicate Arch as viewed from its western side. *Roger Arave photo.*

To access Arches before 1939, today's back entrance, still a dirt road—far north of today's main entrance—was often used. The current entrance, off Highway 191 at a low point of what was then known as Moab Canyon, was then built steeply up the mountain side. That road was extended in 1948 to reach past Delicate Arch and to Devil's Garden. By 1958, that road was paved. However, it would be the late 1980s before the side road to the Delicate Arch trailhead and, then, to the lookout, was also paved.

PART II

UTAH'S SUPERNATURAL WORLD

12

BIGFOOT IN THE BEEHIVE STATE

There are more Bigfoot sightings in Utah than most people realize. When was the first Bigfoot sighting in Utah? The first universally recognized, publicly reported sighting by the media happened on August 22, 1977, in the High Uintas Wilderness area just a few days after it happened. (There had been a few earlier sightings, but they were reported many years after the fact and did not involve the number of witnesses and detail this one did.)

Two men from North Ogden City and six teenagers claimed they saw a "gorilla-like" creature matching the standard description of a Bigfoot.

Bert Strand, outdoor editor for the *Ogden Standard-Examiner*, a daily newspaper, published an account from the group on August 25, 1977. Jay Barker, a big-game hunter and operator of a trout farm in North Ogden, estimated the creature to be ten feet tall and "covered with a white mantle of hair over its shoulders and half-way down its huge body." The creature's lower portion was dark in color, and it moved away on its hind legs.

This sighting took place as the group looked down from the top of a ridge in Summit County, located between Cuberant Basin and Pass Lake. The elevation in this area is well over ten thousand feet above sea level.

Being about six miles from their vehicle, the group was deep in a wilderness area with heavy timber. All eight members of the party watched in disbelief as the creature walked around a small lake, about one mile below the eleven-thousand-foot-elevation ridge they stood on. Barker thought at first it might be an elk. However, after one of the boys knocked some loose rocks that rolled down, the creature turned and looked up at them. "What are we looking at?" Larry Beeson asked in surprise.

Above: A sign by Utah UFO Hunters was posted at a home in Layton after there were numerous Bigfoot sightings in the spring and summer of 2011. *Author photo.*

Left: This April 1, 1993 (not an April Fool's story) illustration in the *Deseret News* accompanied a lengthy news investigation into Bigfoot sightings in Utah by Lynn Arave. *Author photo of Deseret News Archives.*

Barker admitted that the creature was too far away to get a clear look at its face, but they watched it walk—on two legs—about 880 yards before disappearing in heavy timber.

The party was "dumbfounded" and "amazed." They then went down to where the creature had been and found huge "paw-like" prints on the hard ground. They also found scuff marks on some nearby ground, trees and rocks and a partially eaten rabbit carcass completely "skinned as by a human."

The two men and six boys decided it was unwise to follow the creature into heavy brush. Returning to camp, the group could not sleep and spent the night huddled around their campfire at Fish Lake.

The next day, the party hiked out the six miles to Pass Lake, near the Mirror Lake paved highway and just north of Mirror Lake itself.

The *Standard-Examiner* article also reported that Arlo Fawcett of Roy, a sheepherder in the Gold Hill area to the north, reported that his sheep had been uneasy at the same time. They were filled with fear and would not stay in a grazing area where they were led, the same area where the group had spotted the creature. The sheep raced back to camp, not wanting to remain at the grazing area.

Fawcett said he'd never seen sheep act like that. Unlike previous summers spent there, he failed to hear any coyotes in the region.

Jerry Dahlberg, a conservation officer for the Utah Division of Wildlife Resources, responded to the tale of the creature by stating that it sounded like a grizzly bear sighting, except for the long distance the creature walked upright.

Other hikers and fishermen came forward after hearing about this sighting and said that two weeks prior they had heard strange howls and growling in that area of Cuberant Basin. The sounds were unlike anything they'd experienced before. Barker returned to the area a week later and reported a strange smell.

This solid-sounding tale of the creature attracted the interest of many Bigfoot enthusiasts in the United States. The *Davis News Journal* reported that for three weeks after the initial sighting in the Uintas, scores of people scoured the area in search of the elusive creature. Weber County sent an official search party to the area, accompanied by Officer Dahlberg, but found nothing conclusive.

Despite searching ten square miles, nothing was found. The group even searched an additional area, the Bear River side of the region. Dahlberg said that some of the search area was "so primitive it looked like it had never before been penetrated by man." He hoped to have found a form of shelter

The lofty High Uinta Mountains have been the scene of many Bigfoot sightings in Utah. This photo is looking northward from Bald Mountain. *Author photo.*

used by the creature, animal carcasses or torn trees, but nothing along those lines was discovered.

Even earlier than the sighting by Barker, two middle-aged couples from Bountiful and Hill Air Force Base reported seeing not one but three Bigfoot-like creatures in the Uintas that summer of 1977.

Mr. and Mrs. Robert Melka and Sergeant and Mrs. Fred Rosenberg spoke exclusively to the *Davis County Clipper* of their experience on July 10 in the High Uintas, about one half mile southwest of Elizabeth Lake and approximately seventeen miles northwest of the Barker group sighting: "We sat on a ridge looking into a meadow only 300 to 500 yards away when we saw the first creature," said Robert Melka. "A few seconds later, a second beast—both much larger than humans—entered the meadow and the two romped back and forth in the clearing for at least ten minutes."

The couples' descriptions seemed uniform—beasts with hair on their bodies except for their hands and feet. They walked upright, but their arms and legs seemed longer than humans'. They were easily eight to ten feet tall.

Two of the beasts romped and played in a meadow while the third stood nearby. The two couples believe the creatures could not see their position up on a secluded ridge. "They did not have pointed snouts as bears do and we had a good, long look at their profiles," Sergeant Rosenberg noted. A wild-game hunter for more than a quarter century, Rosenberg said, "These were nothing like anything I have seen before, in real life or otherwise."

About a century earlier, at the timber camp in Ephraim Canyon during the early construction of the Manti LDS Church Temple (likely in the late 1870s), there was an incident one night in which men of the camp were terrified by a creature in the forest. It made strange noises, killed some of their dogs and frightened their horses. They finally started a bonfire and shot off guns in the darkness to try to get it to leave. It did finally depart.

Some believe this creature was a Bigfoot, making this possibly the first recorded sighting of Sasquatch in Utah Territory.

Perhaps the second Bigfoot sighting in Utah took place in the late nineteenth century in the Tuschar Mountains east of Beaver. There's a canyon in the western slopes of these mountains, which stand more than twelve thousand feet high. The canyon is strangely called Gorilla Canyon. Nearby is a Gorilla Ridge and a Gorilla Creek. Why the gorilla name? In most local histories, the tale is told of miners who mistook one of their own unshaven prospectors at dusk for a gorilla.

It sounds more than odd that such a minor incident would produce three permanent place-names in the area. Some southern Utah residents don't buy that explanation and believe it to be the sanitized version. They suspect a Bigfoot sighting, more than a half century before that term was even coined, to be a more likely prospect. (Gorillas were sometimes credited in nineteenth-century Sasquatch sightings.)

Otherwise, the earliest reported Bigfoot sighting in Utah may have been sometime in the early 1970s in Clarkston, Cache County. During a 1981 conversation with a former Miss Cache County, then living in Logan, strange tales and eventually Bigfoot came up. The young woman said that she had grown up in Clarkston, northwest of Logan, and that something both strange and terrible stomped through town late one night. Residents were awakened and frightened by screams.

Another possible Bigfoot incident, reported in the 1980s, happened in 1973. Craig R. Johnson of Farr West, Weber County, was elk hunting with friends in the Manti–La Sal Mountains east of Moab. After returning to camp, they reported that something very powerful had lifted the door off a three-hundred-pound horse trailer and tossed it ten feet away. An imprint in the dust on the door didn't indicate a bear or a human but something unknown.

In April 1977, some children in the town of Washington, in Utah's Dixie/ St. George area, reported seeing a mammoth creature lurking through the town's streets. Later, strange footprints were found in the same area on many different nights.

February 3–4, 1980, in South Weber, Utah, was a time like no other in the Beehive State. Multiple sightings of Bigfoot were reported. The city was abuzz with chatter. Sightings would continue through the first part of that month.

First, Pauline Markham said she spotted a big, black creature in broad daylight at about 2:30 p.m. on February 3. The creature was coming down the ridge and toward the Davis-Weber Canal. Then, at about 12:20 a.m. on February 4, Ronald Smith, who had just gotten home from work, went out in the yard to feed his horse. The animal would not come to the fence to feed and was acting strange. Then Smith heard something in the field. It was a moonlit night, and he saw what he first thought was a teenager trying to enter his property. But it screamed four times, like a cougar but much louder, and he then realized not only that the figure was much larger than a person but also that he needed to get in the house.

The next day, Smith found large barefoot tracks—some of them six feet apart—in his field, though his horse had trampled through most of them.

Other strange footprints were found all over the area in the coming days. Sadly, the media reports on the sightings didn't appear until more than a week after they occurred. The reporter who covered the sightings, apparently days afterward, admitted that he was a skeptic. But he said that he had never seen footprints like those.

Edna Arave, the author's aunt, of South Weber said she didn't see anything that night, but she did hear some weird screams. She described them as unlike anything she'd heard before—cries that chilled you to the bone.

Her report was typical of many residents—not wanting to talk about what they saw or heard unless prodded. It is certain that many sightings or experiences were never reported for fear of ridicule.

It was almost three weeks later, on February 24, 1980, that a motorist on Riverdale Road, Lee Padilla of Clearfield, claimed to have seen Bigfoot run across the road at 3:30 a.m. "It had long legs, a head like a gorilla with long, dark brown furry hair that was in layers," Padilla said. He estimated the creature to be ten or more feet tall and that it had no fear or concern for his approaching vehicle.

Darrell Duane Smith of Sandy, Utah, a Bigfoot researcher, created this original Bigfoot costume, with a devilish accent. Smith had a strong interest in Sasquatch for decades. Although he never claimed to have seen the elusive creature, he based the costume on his research from eyewitness reports. *Courtesy of Darrell Duane Smith.*

Another Bigfoot photograph with the costume created by Darrell Duane Smith of Sandy, Utah. Smith had fun with the costume, but he genuinely believed that the creature exists and even roams the territory of Utah. Sadly, Smith died on March 23, 2012, of Lou Gehrig's disease at the age of sixty-seven. *Courtesy of Darrell Duane Smith.*

The Riverdale sighting set off a firestorm of fear about the creature. "Armed 'Bigfoot' Hunters Not Wanted in Riverdale," read a headline in the *Ogden Standard-Examiner* on March 1, 1980. The Riverdale Police chief, Michael Daily, was tired of reports of armed men cruising the city looking for the creature. "We've been getting calls like you wouldn't believe," Chief Daily said.

In one incident, an armed resident searching for the beast turned out to be a boy with a BB gun—though the kid was looking for Bigfoot.

A *Standard-Examiner* headline of February 14, 1980, read, "Men Claim Bigfoot Hair Found." That article included a Mountain Green resident reporting an awful odor one night in February—not a skunk, but something different. The article also reported that a South Weber woman, Mrs. Walter G. Ray, said that a pot of stew she put outside to cool on the night of February 13 was hauled one hundred yards away and licked clean. The Rays also found weird, bearlike tracks around their yard and said that their dogs had been acting strangely that night.

In other weeks in February and March 1980, some kids claimed they saw a Bigfoot by the Ogden River and Twelfth Street. Other young persons had sightings near Cold Water Canyon in the North Ogden area. These incidents put northern Utah on the Bigfoot map.

Despite all of these sightings, some South Weber residents of the early 1980s, like Darrin Cuttler, believed it was probably a bear that ran through the town and are not convinced it was a Bigfoot, if that even exists.

(The author's Google blog, sasqwasatch.blogspot.com, contains a running list of purported Bigfoot sightings in Utah, with more than 130 possible incidents reported.)

The High Uintas, Ogden Valley and North Ogden have the most total sightings in Utah. Those three areas have more than 42 percent of the state's sightings. Bigfoot sightings in northern Utah continue every year.

Note, too, that Utah is definitely a major part of the world's supernatural puzzle these days, and not just because of Bigfoot. The mysterious Skinwalker Ranch is also located in the Beehive State, southeast of Roosevelt.

13

BEAR LAKE MONSTER

The rough equivalent in Utah and Idaho of the Loch Ness Monster is the Bear Lake Monster. It dates back to Native American legends and was first reported by pioneer settlers in the summer of 1868. The single mass sighting included ten different creatures.

"Monsters of Bear Lake" ran an August 5, 1868 headline in the *Deseret News* (Utah's only newspaper at the time). Correspondence from Charles C. Rich, namesake of Rich County and an LDS Church apostle, comprised this initial monster report, given almost five years after settlers had first arrived there.

The "monsters" around Bear Lake then were listed as, first, grasshopper swarms and crop destroyers and, second, the Bear Lake Monster, an elusive sea creature.

The Bear Lake Monster reference is highly significant, occurring ninety years before the term *Bigfoot* was coined. It came sixty-five years before the famed Loch Ness Monster became known worldwide (though some Loch sightings may date to the seventh century).

"All lakes, caves and dens have their legendary histories," Rich wrote. "Tradition loves to throw her magic wand over beautiful dells and lakes, and people them with fairies, giants and monsters of various kinds. Bear Lake has also its own monster tale to tell, and when I have told it, I will leave you to judge whether or no ["not"] its merits are merely traditionary."

Rich continued:

The Indians say there is a monster animal that lives in the Lake that has captured and carried away Indians while in the Lake swimming; but they say it has not been seen by them for many years, not since the buffalo inhabited the valley. They represent it as being of the serpent kind, but having legs about eighteen inches long on which they sometimes crawl out of the water a short distance on the shore. They also say its spirits water upwards out of its mouth.

So, it is likely that Native Americans hadn't sighted the local lake monster for more than two decades before the pioneers arrived.

Rich's 1868 newspaper account continued: "Since the settlement of this valley, several persons have reported seeing a huge animal of some kind that they could not describe; but such persons have generally been alone when they saw it, and but little credence has been attached to the monster, and until this summer the 'monster question' had about died out."

There were two other pre-1868 Bear Lake Monster sightings by early settlers.

Bear Lake, with half of its brilliant blue waters in Utah, is home to the purported Bear Lake Monster. The first recorded sightings were in 1868. *Author photo.*

Rich next reported:

About three weeks ago [likely early July 1868], *Mr. S.M. Johnson, who lives in the east side of the lake at a place called South Eden* [about halfway north along the Utah side of the lake], *was going to the Round Valley settlement, six miles to the south of this place and when about half way he saw something in the lake, which at the time, he thought to be a drowned person. The road being some distance from the water's edge he rode to the bench, and as the waves were running pretty high he thought it would soon wash into shore. In a few minutes two or three feet of some kind of animal that he had never seen before were raised out of the water.*

The report continued:

He did not see the body, only the head and what he supposed to be part of the neck. It had ears or bunches on the side of its head nearly as large as a pint cup. The waves at times would dash over its head, when it would throw water from its mouth or nose. It did not drift landward but appeared stationary, with the exception of turning its head. Mr. Johnson thought a portion of the body must lie on the bottom of the lake or it would have drifted with the action of water. This is Mr. Johnson's version as he told me.

The report of a monster expelling water seems consistent with Native American stories. The deepest part of Bear Lake, about 209 feet, is not far from there, also on the east side.

Rich wrote that the next day three women spotted a similar monster in the same place along the lake. It was "very large and [some] say it swam much faster than a horse could run on land."

"These recent discoveries again revived the 'monster question,'" Rich reported. "Those who had seen it before brought in their claims anew, and many people began to think this story was not altogether moonshine."

Rich then recounted more sightings:

On Sunday last [July 19, 1868], *N.C. Davis and Alan Davis of St. Charles and Thomas Slight and J. Collings of Paris with six women, were returning from Fish Haven, when about midway from the latter named place to St. Charles* [all in today's borders of Idaho], *their attention was suddenly attracted to a peculiar motion or wave in the water, about three miles distant. The lake was not rough, only a little disturbed by a light wind. Mr. Slight says he distinctly saw the sides of a very large animal that he would suppose to not be less than ninety feet in length....It was going south and all agreed that it swam with a speed almost incredible to their senses. Mr. Davis says he never saw a locomotive travel faster, and thinks it made a mile a minute, easy.*

The 1868 report continued: "In a few minutes after the discovery of the first, a second one followed in its wake; but seemed to be much smaller, appearing to Mr. Slight about the size of a horse. A larger one followed this, and so one until four large ones, in all, and six small ones had run southward out of sight."

Rich then attested to Mr. Davis and Mr. Slight as being well-known and reliable persons. "I have no doubt they would be willing to make affidavits to their statement," Rich wrote. "There you have the monster story so far as completed, but I hope it will be concluded by the capture of one sometime. If so large an animal exists in this altitude, and in so small a lake, what can it be? It must be something new under the sun."

Rich concluded his report by stating that some settlers were talking of uniting to form a company to try to capture the monster, as it was something to rival P.T. Barnum's attractions (of later worldwide circus fame).

There were more Bear Lake Monster sightings in 1870. A report in 1907 claimed that the elusive sea monster had devoured a horse.

Modern Bear Lake Monster sightings are a rarity. There were many encounters between 1868 and 1915, but they diminished substantially after that forty-seven-year period. Did the monster retire, slumber, die or move away?

There are other Bear Lakes in other states. For example, California has a Bear Lake. But only the Bear Lake in Utah and Idaho seems to have had monster sightings.

A young child claimed to have seen the monster in 1937, and a Boy Scout leader sighted it in 1946. A tale of scuba divers spotting something

---

A BEAR LAKE MONSTER SEEN ON LAKE SHORE

Swims Seven and a Half Miles In One Hour. Ranchers Unable to Capture Animal

Mr. Smyth the horseman, just returned from Bear Lake and has a good story to tell. It resembles the Bear Lake Monster story in many respects. He says a few days ago a range rider ran across a large Bull Moose north of the Hot Springs and pursued it as far south as the Hot Springs when it took to the lake and began to swim across to the Fish Haven side. Ranchers were phoned of the event and they went out with horses and saddles and attempted to rope the animal when he arrived on the west side of the lake, but he was too clever for them.

After surrounding the animal with an attempt to capture it, the bull moose broke through the trap and made to the hills to the west. Mr. Smythe says it took just one hour for the moose to swim the distance of seven and a half miles.

"Bear Lake Monster News." Logan Republican, *October, 7, 1915. Digitized by J. Willard Marriott Library, University of Utah.*

The Bear Lake Monster Shop in St. Charles, Idaho, is one of several businesses with references to the elusive lake monster around Bear Lake. *Author photo.*

large under the water in the late 1970s is another of these stories. One of the spooked divers claimed he'd never go under the water again at that lake.

A Murray man said he was boating on the east side of the lake with family in 1985 when they saw what could have only been a large creature swimming in the lake. It quickly disappeared, but bubbles continued to come to the surface for a few minutes afterward. He said in 2017 that he has no doubt the Bear Lake Monster is real.

A Bear Lake Valley businessman reported seeing it in 2002. No known sightings of the Bear Lake Monster were reported from 2006 to the spring of 2022.

Reflecting the public's fascination with the monster, drawings of the creature are spotted on a few buildings in the Bear Lake Valley. Some businesses make use of the monster in their names, and some restaurants have menu items named for the Bear Lake Monster.

In the early twenty-first century, there was even a short-lived tourist boat named after the lake monster.

Note: One of the author's Google blogs contains much more information on the Bear Lake Monster: bearlakemonsterlegend.blogspot.com.

14

GREAT SALT LAKE MONSTER

Does the Great Salt Lake harbor a large sea monster? If it does, the creature rarely gets out. The only time it was seen was on the night of July 8, 1877.

According to the *Salt Lake Herald* of July 13, 1877, a group of men saw the beast near Monument Point. They then fled far away.

Bear Lake, straddling the Utah-Idaho border, has had its share of monster tales, but the GSL beast has just a single story. Monument Point, where the monster was supposedly seen, is in the extreme northwest corner of the Great Salt Lake. (That's northwest of Promontory Point.)

The men reported seeing "a huge mass of hide and fin rapidly approaching and when within a few yards of the shore it raised its enormous head and uttered a terrible bellow." The men fled to the mountains and did not return until the next morning. They reported finding some overturned rocks, torn-up ground and tracks on the shore.

One of the men, J.H. McNeil, said the beast had to be some seventy-five feet long and was like an alligator or crocodile, only much larger. The men,

A "Monster" Story.

A correspondent of the Corinne Record, sends that paper a graphic account of the discovery at Monument Point, of a large monster in Great Salt Lake. The discovery is said to have been made by the night hands at Barnes & Co.'s salt boilers, on the night of the 8th. The story, briefly, is that strange noises proceeding from the lake have been frequently heard. On the night in question, the men saw "a huge mass of hide and fin rapidly approaching, and when within a few yards of the shore it raised its enormous head and uttered a terrible bellow." The men took to their heels, fleeing to the mountains and did not return until daylight, when the trail of the animal was traced. Rocks were found to have been turned over by the monster, and the ground had been torn up by it. J. H. McNeil, one of the men who claim to have seen the monster, makes affidavit to his story, in which he says it was "a great animal like a crocodile or alligator, approaching the bank, but much larger than I had ever heard of one being. It must have been seventy-five feet long, but the head was not like an alligator's—it was more like a horse's. When within a few yards of the shore it made a loud noise and my companion and I fled up the mountain, where we stayed all night. When we came down in the morning we saw tracks on the shore, but nothing else."

The story is probably a hoax; however, the editor of the Record vouches for the correspondent as "a man whose veracity cannot be impeached."

Opposite: Salt Lake Herald-Republican, *July 13, 1877.*

Above: The north end of the Great Salt Lake is where the sightings of a lake monster began in 1877. This view is from Fremont Island looking north. *Author photo.*

night employees at Barnes and Company's salt boilers, also reported hearing strange noises from the lake just before the encounter.

The newspaper stated that many claimed the sighting to be a hoax but that McNeil "is a man whose veracity cannot be impeached."

Unlike Bear Lake, the Great Salt Lake is a very shallow body of water. At Monument Point, the lake is only 2 to 4 feet deep anywhere near the shore—and that's when the GSL is at its average elevation of 4,200 feet above sea level. As of 2021, the area where this sighting took place is dry, the lake being down almost 9 feet from average.

OTHER UTAH MONSTERS

Tales of the Bear Lake Monster are well known in Utah, but how about the Stansbury Lake Monster of the Great Salt Lake and the Panguitch Lake Monster? These are two separate lake creatures that in the past generated their own legends.

THE STANSBURY ISLAND MONSTER

"Monster That Swims and Flies Sighted on Stansbury Island Shores," was a July 30, 1903 headline in the *Salt Lake Telegram.* Martin Gilbert and John Barry were two Utah hunters who claimed to have spotted the creature at the south end of the lake. They said it was some sixty-five feet long, with an alligator-like head, spiny scales on its body and wings than spanned one hundred feet.

The men saw the creature fly and eat a horse whole. They shot at it, but all that resulted was salt crystals raining down on them, as if the monster had armor of crystal salt. They tracked the creature to a cave but dared not enter. Soon, the creature flew away. When it came back about an hour later, it had a mangled horse in its mouth. After eating, it entered the lake waters and swam northward until it disappeared.

Although the *Herald* newspaper gave the initial report without skepticism, the following day was different. The *Herald* on August 1, 1903, reported:

MONSTER THAT SWIMS AND FLIES IS SIGHTED ON STANSBURY ISLAND SHORES

Hunters Tell a Wild and Woolly Story of Beast That Wears an Armor of Crystal Salt.

A terrible, nameless, unclassified creature of the animal world is exciting the curiosity, wonder and fear of occasional visitors to Stansbury island. In the

WHAT MONSTER IS SAID TO LOOK LIKE.

HEAD: Like an alligator's, nearly fifteen feet in length.
MOUTH: Armed with immense serrated teeth, opening wide enough to admit a horse.
BODY: Presumably scaly, but so incrusted with salt that it cannot b. seen.
EYES: Very large, round and burning with a bright red light.
WINGS: Bat-like, spreading probably 100 feet from tip to tip.

Salt Lake Telegram, July 20, 1903.

> *The monster, the two hunters described carried enough salt encrusted on its body for every person who read their tale to have accepted the story with several grains of salt. However, the impression that one of the imaginative nimrods is none other than Walt McDougall, who writes strange animal stories and draws wonderful pictures for the children, is growing daily.*
> *—Editor the Herald.*

These two references are all there is to the Stansbury creature.

THE PANGUITCH LAKE MONSTER

The *Salt Lake Herald* of September 21, 1878, carried the headline "A Lake Legend: The Monster of Panguitch Lake: What the Indians Say of Him, His Coming and His Going."

The story recounts a lengthy Native American tale of the lake monster in which the beast killed one hundred Indian maidens. One warrior vowed vengeance and eventually stormed the lake with thousands of warriors. The beast fled southward in a great flood and was eventually swallowed up in the earth at the sink of the Sevier River.

A July 4, 1891 story in the *Deseret Weekly* newspaper stated that Panguitch Lake cannot boast of its monsters, like Bear Lake, because it has none.

In addition to the monsters already mentioned, there are tales of a Sevier Lake Monster, so named because that's where the Panguitch Lake Monster supposedly went. (In recent decades, there has been no water there.) There is also the tale of a Utah Lake Monster.

One of the first reports of the Utah Lake creature surfaced in August 1868, shortly after the initial sighting of the Bear Lake Monster. Henry Walker of Lehi was in Utah Lake in 1864 when, "to his fear and surprise, he saw what looked like a large snake…with the head of a greyhound," historian D. Robert Carter said.

In the late 1860s, two men reported seeing splashing in the Jordan River and Utah Lake. They spotted a creature with a head shaped like a grayhound and having "wicked-looking black eyes."

The *Deseret News* reported on the majority of these monster sightings, but Carter said the newspaper at one time accused Utah Valley residents of simply creating a character for Utah Lake. Another newspaper, the *Daily Corrine* in Box Elder County, said that all of the sightings were sheer fabrications and that the monster actually lived at the north end of the Great Salt Lake, as evidenced by recent sightings there.

Carter said during a presentation at the Utah State Historical Society's forty-ninth annual meeting that he suspects the monster might represent modifications to the local Indians' belief in "water babies," dwarfs who sounded like crying babies and who would lure mortals into the water. While this belief may have helped the Native Americans explain drownings, pioneer settlers didn't want to believe in such myths. Snakelike monsters in the lakes were much more acceptable to them.

The *Deseret News* reported in the early 1870s that lake monsters were becoming fashionable but that by the 1880s they had fallen out of favor. Carter said they were then akin to a large species of bug "known as hum-bug." There was one sighting and a brief upsurge in 1921 of the Utah Lake Monster, but then it "sank in the depths of the lake" and apparently hasn't been seen since.

Though we more readily scoff at these monster tales today, Carter said that even the 1870s were not without some unbelievers.

The Utah Lake monster, as one example, may not be an intentional lie, he said. Rather, the legend is likely based on illusion and imagination—"and," Carter said, "a dearth of good optometrists."

Add up all the Utah sea monsters—ten at Bear Lake in the initial report and those recounted here—and there are at least fifteen total monsters in five different bodies of water.

There is also a strange tale of a flying monster: "Flying Serpent Terrifies Early Ogden Valley Residents: A Veritable Eden. The Serpent Is at His Old Tricks Again," reported the July 23, 1894 *Ogden Standard-Examiner*. This was from the Eden of Weber County, in Ogden Valley. On the previous Friday

Eden, Utah, on the north side of Pineview Reservoir, was the location of the sighting of a monstrous flying serpent in 1894. *Author photo.*

evening about sundown, "a number of Eden's reliable men" claimed they spotted a "monster serpent" one hundred feet long and eighteen inches in diameter flying through the air and swooping down near Wilbur's Store, near Independence Park.

They estimated it was moving at between thirty-six and forty miles per hour and soon disappeared over the mountains in the direction of Middle Fork, apparently never to be spotted again.

A serpent in biblically named Eden, just this side of Paradise (on the north side in Cache County)—who knew?

"Flying Creature Shocks Trainmen: The Mother of a Son Who Worked for Union Pacific Told This Chilling Tale." In about 2005, the son and another Union Pacific engineer were railroading their usual route from Ogden to Elko, Nevada. Both men claimed to have clearly spotted a flying creature zip in front of the train and speed away. It was clear and massive, like a giant jellyfish. Both men were shocked, never having seen anything like it in decades of driving trains. This happened out by Lakeside, along the border of the west side of the Great Salt Lake.

They claimed to have spotted the same flying creature on their return trip to Ogden in the same area. They said it was a living entity, not a drone or aircraft.

The December 25, 1873 *Deseret News* contains the tale ("Giant Snake in the Oquirrh Mountains") of a monster snake in the right-hand fork of Coon's Canyon, southwest of Salt Lake City. A man, Edward R. Walker, was felling timber on a high peak south of Black Rock when a deer ran by. Walker grabbed his rifle and decided to pursue. A mile later, the sound of a shrill whistle and hiss interrupted his chase.

Walker's report stated: "He saw approaching him, at a very rapid rate, a serpent, which he judged was between thirty and forty feet long, and about 10 inches through the body. The reptile's head was raised fully six feet from the ground and his jaws were open fifteen or eighteen inches wide, with fangs growing from both upper and lower jaw."

The snake chased him. Walker soon stumbled and felt the weight of the monster's body gliding over his. Then the snake seemed to become frightened and slid off at a tremendous rate toward the ridge of the mountain. Walker said the snake was yellow and covered with scales. He said he would never set foot in that canyon again, despite having had years of experience in the mountains.

"'Gorilla' Man Attacks Woman and S.L. Street" was a December 18, 1931 headline in the *Salt Lake Telegram*. This beast ripped the woman's clothes off after violently hurling her to the ground. The woman said the man, sporting shaggy hair, was frothing at the mouth, mumbling insanely, had an iron grip and was walking in an apelike manner. This attack took place at State Street and Downington Avenue. Police believe this same man molested a dozen small girls on the city's west side, but they were unable to locate him. No more sightings of him were ever reported.

THREE NEPHITES IN UTAH

Elder Orson Pratt was the first leader in the Church of Jesus Christ of Latter-day Saints to call attention to the famed "Three Nephites" to the general church. This apostle did so on April 7, 1855, in a sermon at the new bowery in Salt Lake City. (In LDS Church theology, the "Three Nephites" are translated beings, like John the Revelator from the New Testament. They cannot die and are beyond the powers of earth. They will remain on earth until Jesus Christ returns.)

In his sermon, Elder Pratt said that these heavenly beings can show themselves to whomever they choose. Otherwise, they remain unseen. He said they come among us openly because the time is not right and there is work for humans to do to prepare to Christ's return. They work in secret to promote righteousness.

Elder Erastus Snow and President Brigham Young also gave sermons that alluded to the existence of these Three Nephites. But Elder James E. Talmage, an LDS apostle in the early twentieth century, said that church members in his era were too eager to attribute any unusual happening to the Three Nephites. As such, he said they must be the most overworked of all individuals.

In recent times, it has been assumed that, since physical struggles are less of an issue for us today, we don't have the need for these individuals, at least for physical matters.

In many of the tales of visits by these beings, they are described as old men with white hair and beards. In various stories from Utah over the decades,

Orson Pratt. *Public domain, L. Tom Perry Special Collections, Harold B. Lee Library, Brigham Young University.*

the beings range from ghostly hitchhikers who appear, offer spiritual advice and eventually disappear from a car's back seat, to beggars who ask for food to test our generosity.

In others, someone is saved from death. For example, in the 1950s, a young boy fell into deep water at the Ogden Bay Bird Refuge, located west of Hooper. He might have drowned had not an older man appeared out of nowhere to save him. The man then vanished.

In another tale, two young girls were hiking in the mountains around Richfield in the early twentieth century. They became lost, then a man appeared and led them back to the trail before disappearing.

Some of these stories are contained in a 1947 PhD dissertation by Hector Lee, "The Three Nephites: The Substance and Significance of the Legend in Folklore."

GADIANTON ROBBERS ROOSTED HERE

Did the infamous Gadianton Robbers of the Book of Mormon (Helaman 6:18–29) inhabit western U.S. mountains? Yes, they did, and even in the Wasatch Mountains, according to Brigham Young:

> *There are scores of evil spirits here—spirits of the old Gadianton robbers, some of whom inhabited these mountains, and used to go into the south and afflict the Nephites. There are millions of those spirits in these mountains, and they are ready to make us covetous, if they can; they are ready to lead astray every man and woman that wishes to be a Latter-day Saint. (Journal of Discourses, 8:344, from a discourse by President Young on January 20, 1861, in the Tabernacle of Salt Lake City.)*

The Gadianton Robbers is a group of organized, evil men mentioned in the Book of Mormon. They take secret oaths administered by Satan to murder, rob, destroy freedom and persecute believers in Christ.

Another Gadianton Robber tale comes from a trip to southeast Deseret territory by W.D. Huntington and twelve other men, including one Indian, in 1854 by a request from Brigham Young. This group of explorers found extensive Indian ruins that the current (at that time) Native Americans said they didn't build and that were very old. It is estimated that the group was about five hundred miles southeast of Salt Lake City. The men were quoted in the *Deseret News* of December 28, 1854: "We very readily came to a conclusion drawn from the Book of Mormon in second Chapter of

The Wasatch Mountains (*far background*) were said to be where Gadianton Robbers hid out in the times of the Book of Mormon. This view is looking northwest from the Uintas. *Author photo.*

the book of Nephi that the ancient possessors of these strongholds were robbers of the Gadianton band and we considered this locality as one of their strongholds."

According to the *Daily Spectrum* of May 9, 1976, there were tales of Gadianton Robbers living in that area in past times. There was an early sawmill in Pine Valley that was plagued by broken saws, disappearing tools and general bad luck. The matter was supposedly taken to Brigham Young, who said the mill was on a site where some Gadianton Robbers had been buried centuries earlier. He suggested moving the mill to another location and the problems would be solved. Apparently, that solution worked.

PART III

HISTORICAL BEEHIVE MYTHS

18
SALT LAKE NOT TREELESS
IN 1847

How did the myth, originating in 1847 with the arrival of Mormon pioneers, of the lack of trees in the Salt Lake Valley begin?

Richard Jackson, professor of geography at Brigham Young University, said that this idea developed in later years, probably for three reasons.

> *First, as the settlers celebrated the 24th of July, the oratory often included a certain amount of hyperbole about the magnitude of the trip across the plains, settling and developing the Salt Lake Valley, etc. As with most reminiscences, the story tends to grow with the retelling, so the Salt Lake Valley became ever more arid in those accounts.*
>
> *Secondly, by the 1850s and 1860s when these myths became common, the only land not being farmed or built upon was in fact the worst land that was more arid and so later arrivals concluded that the entire valley found in 1847 by the pioneers was basically the same as the remaining marginal lands in the valley.*
>
> *Thirdly, as Brigham Young and the leaders encouraged the settlers to go south to Dixie, etc., the idea that Salt Lake Valley was a treeless desert implied that the farms and city that the settlers had developed with the help of the Lord could be replicated in the more marginal sites he was encouraging settlers to move to.*

The late Stanley Kimball, a Utah historian, once said he also believed it came about—consciously or subconsciously—after the desirable valley filled up, thus fostering the idea that it had been tamed and to encourage people to settle in Dixie and other frontier areas.

Left: The Lone Cedar Tree monument in Salt Lake City, in the median on the south side of the intersection at 600 East and 300 South Streets. *Author photo.*

Above: The Lone Cedar Tree monument indirectly helps perpetuate the myth of a treeless Salt Lake Valley when the pioneers arrived. *Author photo.*

Besides paintings, the biggest myth supporter is perhaps the Lone Cedar Tree monument in Salt Lake City, located in the median on the south side of the intersection at 600 East and 300 South Streets.

The Daughters of the Utah Pioneers (DUP) erected this monument on Pioneer Day in 1934 in honor of what was supposedly the only cedar tree in the valley when the 1847 pioneers arrived. Some original pioneers are believed to have sung hymns and prayed by the tree. One problem with the story is that the pioneers followed the Donner Party trail to about 1700 South Street, then headed to a small grove of cottonwood trees near today's 300 South State Street, thus missing the "Lone Cedar Tree."

Vandals cut the Lone Cedar Tree down on September 21, 1958. A related controversy ensued with the DUP, when the media said the tree's status was a fraud anyway. (Ashes from the stolen cedar tree were purportedly later found in a Greyhound bus depot locker.)

A new plaque was added to the monument in 1960 and is still there today for anyone to see and decide for themselves if the tree's legendary status holds merit.

UTAH'S SIX PRE-PIONEER RESIDENTS IN 1847

Most histories of early Utah would have you assume that Miles Goodyear was the lone non–Native American living in Utah territory when the Mormon pioneers arrived in 1847. But there may have been as many as five other non-Indians living in the region before the pioneers, making a total of six.

Details on these men are sketchy, but here is what is known about several of them, according to a *Deseret News* article from December 15, 1906, under the headline "Utah Legends, Indians, Trappers and Pioneers." A mountain man, Peg Leg Smith, was living in the Bear Lake Valley (partially in Utah) before the pioneers arrived. He told the settlers many Native American tales about Bear Lake and operated a trading post at Dingle, Idaho, on the north end of the valley.

Two brothers by the last name of Goodall operated a horse and goat ranch in the Ogden "Flats" area and may have been bought out by Mormon settlers, as Goodyear was.

William H. Kimball, Heber C. Kimball's oldest son, was sent by Brigham Young in 1848 to buy out the Goodalls. They apparently had 750 horses grazing on ten square miles. Kimball moved the horses to Antelope Island ("Church Island"). Although no purchase price to the Goodalls was recorded, they told Kimball they had secured the land from Mexicans, who had started a mission there.

The younger Kimball had also reported that a Mexican man named Gibo had discovered a small Spanish fort in southwest Ogden, complete with a safe that contained some coins.

The Miles Goodyear Cabin, built about 1845, is Utah's oldest structure. This photograph is dated to when it resided on Tabernacle Square in Ogden, moved from Fort Buenaventura. *Daughters of Utah Pioneers photo.*

Barney Ward was mentioned as another mountaineer who was living in the Ogden area when the pioneers arrived. He dealt in tobacco and liquor sales, products not much in demand by Mormon settlers.

Finally, "Daddy Stump," another non-Indian, was living on Antelope Island when the Mormon pioneers started exploring the island in 1848. That's also the first mention of the man. Stump, believed to be a mountain man and perhaps also known as a bear killer, had built a small cabin and had a small orchard of peaches on Antelope Island (from the LDS *Improvement Era* magazine of March 1907).

Daddy Stump has other historical references, as does Peg Leg Smith, but the other men remain mysterious, with just a single mention in history. Sadly, the 1906 *Deseret News* article did not list its source or sources on the men's existence. Assuming that there is some accuracy to the account, the area was certainly not quite as deserted when the pioneers arrived as is so often envisioned.

In addition, an Ogden Canyon legend claims it supposedly contained a dugout and a cabin reputed to have been built by Peter Skene Ogden. In addition, Utah had some "pre-pioneers" living in Utah in 1902. They were a brother and a sister from the infamous Donner Party who traveled through Utah in 1846, a year earlier.

"Brother and Sister Who Came to Utah in 1846" was a July 23, 1904 headline in the *Deseret Evening News*. "It is indeed interesting to know that there are now living in Utah two persons who traveled the sites of many Utah settlements one year before the advent of the Pioneers," the newspaper stated.

> *They are Mrs. Lucinda Rhoads Dodge of 1321 East South Temple Street, this city, and Caleb Rhoads, who lives on his ranch in Carbon County, near Price. They are daughter and son of "Father" Thomas Rhoads, who led the section of the Donner Party that escaped hardship and later headed the relief expedition that found the ill-fated immigrants living upon human flesh in the tops of the Sierras.*

In 1902, the brother and sister were believed to be the only remaining survivors of the Donner Party. (In fact, in 1902, only 16 of the original July 1847 Mormon pioneer party of 147 were still alive.)

Dodge was sixty-six years old in 1902, and her parents were members of the Church of Jesus Christ of Latter-day Saints. She said her father was

Today, the Miles Goodyear Cabin sits near Twenty-First Street and Lincoln Avenue in Ogden. *Author photo.*

determined to head west early, to California, where he thought the future home of the church would be. If he was wrong, he would return to where the church settled in the future. "My father was a natural-born pioneer," Dodge said.

She also said that even though her father was working at Sutter's Mill when gold was discovered, he wanted to return to Utah, where church members had settled. And he did, with his family, in 1849. "Coming across the plains from California, we buried innumerable skeletons, the gruesome evidence of Indian massacres, but still we were unharmed. Our family seemed to bear charmed lives," she told the *Evening News*.

Dodge also noted that her brother Caleb was often associated with the remarkable story of a mysterious mine in eastern Utah. The *Evening News* story continued:

> *They used to say that about once a year he would disappear for two weeks or more and return with a sack of gold dust. If so, he has never revealed the whereabouts of the mine, except the known fact that there is a gold-producing property somewhere on the reservation. It has been said that the Indians threatened him with death if he ever revealed the location, but most of these tales are regarded by Mrs. Dodge as largely legendary.*

"I know there is gold on the reservation," Dodge told the *Evening News*; she said she handled a lot of it that her father possessed. She said he brought some of the gold from California, but then people thought they had the secret of a gold mine near Vernal. Dodge stressed that even though some believed her brother still visited that secret mine yearly, he had been an invalid for several years.

She said she had visited the Donner site in the Sierras about fifteen years earlier. She also told the *Evening News* what she knew about some of the hardships that the snowed-in party had endured.

20

JULY 1847

SALT LAKE A FORSAKEN PLACE

N ot every Mormon pioneer expressed excitement over their first view of the Great Salt Lake Valley in July 1847.

For example, one pioneer, Harriet Young, said, "Weak and weary as I am I would rather go a thousand miles farther than remain in such a forsaken place as this" (*Utah in Her Western Setting*, by Milton R. Hunter).

Still, once LDS Church president Brigham Young said the Salt Lake Valley was the right place, all the pioneers accepted that and settled there. (There were 147 members of the July 1847 vanguard pioneer group, including 3 women and 2 children. None of the first group died; all made it safely to the Salt Lake Valley after traveling some 1,031 miles.)

Erastus Snow. *Public domain, L. Tom Perry Special Collections, Harold B. Lee Library, Brigham Young University.*

One pioneer shared an excited response with his first view of the Great Salt Lake Valley. Also, he experienced one of the first confrontations with native wildlife by the pioneers, as he encountered a coiled rattlesnake while trying to get a glimpse of the Great Salt Lake. Erastus Snow recorded this account during his first attempt to glimpse the Great Salt Lake Valley on July 21, 1847, and Hunter shares his words.

Right: The Mormon pioneers glimpsed their first views of the Salt Lake Valley from near this upper This is the Place monument, the original marker. *Author photo*.

Below: While the foothills near the mouth of Emigration Canyon may have appeared green and inviting when the Mormon Pioneers arrived—as they do today—the Salt Lake Valley below did not. *Author photo*.

The thicket down the narrows, at the mouth of the [Emigration] canyon, was so dense that one could not penetrate through it. I crawled for some distance on my hands and knees through the thickets, until I was compelled to return, admonished to by the rattle of a snake, which lay coiled up under my nose, having almost put my hand on him; but as he gave me the friendly warning, I thanked him and retreated. We raised on to a high point south of the narrows, where we got a view of the Great Salt Lake and this valley, and each of us, without saying a word to the other, instinctively, as if by inspiration, raised out hats from our heads, and then, swinging our hats, shouted.

MORMON GOLD
BOUGHT OGDEN

I s the Ogden, Utah area worth $1,950, or about 103 ounces of gold?
Dutch colonists are often said to have purchased all of Manhattan Island in 1626 from local Indians for trinkets and cloth worth only about £1.5 of silver, or perhaps just $24. Jump forward some 221 years from that event, to the Utah Territory in 1847 and a somewhat similar event.

Today's Ogden area was territory already settled by whites when the Mormon pioneers arrived in July 1847. Mountain man Miles Goodyear and his family had built a fort (today's Fort Buenaventura) and cabins in what is present-day West Ogden in 1845–46, before the Mormons arrived.

James Brown, a captain in the Mormon Battalion under the direction of Brigham Young, used Mexican or Spanish gold coins worth about $1,950—earned from service in the battalion—to purchase much of today's Ogden area. That price included an area of about 210 square miles, a fort, seventy-five cattle, seventy-five goats, twelve sheep and six horses (and a "$10 cat," according to some sources) from Goodyear on November, 24, 1847. Where Goodyear got that many cattle is another story.

Based on prices per troy ounce of gold for that era (at least in the weight of gold), the purchase price paid by the Mormons might have equaled about 8.5 pounds (103 ounces) of gold. In today's gold values, what the pioneers paid in gold is worth at least $136,500. (In modern values, that $1,950 is only worth about $47,500.)

The view looking down on the greater Ogden area from atop Mount Ogden is obscured today by high-tech transmitters. Mormon Battalion gold was used by the pioneers to purchase the area from Miles Goodyear. *Author photo*.

This gold was Brown's own money, earned for his service in the Mormon Battalion and from some of his business enterprises in California. (Despite "owning" all of the Ogden area land, Brown never charged any settler for homesteading there.)

Goodyear's deed (claimed with an alleged grant from the Mexican government) described the boundaries as follows: "Commencing at the mouth of Weber Canyon and following the base of the mountains north to the hot springs; thence west to the Salt Lake; thence south along the shore to a point opposite Weber Canyon; thence east to the beginning." By that geography lesson, the purchase likely stretched from Weber Canyon to Ogden Canyon (today's Twelfth Street) and to the Great Salt Lake in between. (There is a hot spring near the Box Elder–Weber County line, but that's northwest, so the purchase boundaries more likely referred to the hot springs at the mouth of Ogden Canyon.)

So the area included not just most of today's Ogden City but also some of West Weber and West Warren, all of West Haven, Hooper, Roy, South Ogden, Riverdale, Washington Terrace and Uintah. Also included would have been some of Davis County—parts of South Weber, Sunset, Clinton, West Point and Hill Air Force Base.

Of course, Goodyear almost certainly had no true deed to the property or even a land grant from Mexico. "So far as the land was concerned he had sold Captain Brown a wooden nutmeg!" is how the book *Beneath Ben Lomond's Peak* summarized the land transaction.

Goodyear was seemingly more than a capable mountain man and was apparently a shrewd salesman and entrepreneur. As he moved out and took his family to Benicia, California, only some scattered Native Americans were left in the area. Goodyear's former home first became known as Brown's Fort, or Brown's Settlement. Soon, Brownsville took hold as the name and continued for several years.

The city was named for Peter Skene Ogden on February 6, 1851, when it was incorporated. Ogden was the brigade leader of the Hudson Bay Fur Company who was in the Ogden Valley in the 1830s. Ironically, he likely never set foot on the front side of the Wasatch Mountains into today's Ogden City. Can you imagine if Brownsville had become the name of today's Ogden?

By 1860, Ogden had a population of 1,463 people but was primarily a farming community. It really took off in 1869 with the establishment of the transcontinental railroad. Soon, Ogden became "Junction City," near where the Union Pacific and Central Pacific Railroads met.

Eventually, the equivalent of today's chamber of commerce adopted the motto "You can't get anywhere without coming to Ogden!" That was true, as all passengers and shipments by train in the Mountain West went through Ogden.

Weber County today boasts more than 260,000 residents, and the portions of Davis County in the Goodyear purchase have many thousands more. The $1,950 "purchase," legally necessary or not, certainly appears to have been a great investment.

PIONEER UTAH'S MULTIPLE INSECT INVASIONS

Perhaps the most famous miracles in Mormon pioneer history occurred in June and July 1848, when the first crops in the Salt Lake Valley were threatened by a plague of insects, what would later be called "Mormon crickets."

Starting in May, the crickets started eating the wheat, corn, beans, pumpkins, cucumbers, squash, melons and other crops—and continued to do so for a month. After many prayers by the pioneers, a white cloud of seagulls flew in during early June and started devouring the crickets. But this was not a one-day event. The birds came daily for about three weeks, eating insects, drinking water and then regurgitating before eating more of the insects. The remainder of the pioneer crops was saved.

This timely appearance of gulls was described in a letter of June 9 to Brigham Young, who was back East at the time: "The sea gulls have come in large flocks from the lake and sweep the crickets as they go; it seems the hand of the Lord is in our favor." (For some pioneer settlers, it apparently required months for this to be heralded as a miracle.) The Seagull Monument on Salt Lake's Temple Square commemorates that event.

Anabrus simplex, the Mormon cricket. *Photo by Lazurus000, Wikicommons (CC BY-SA 4.0).*

The Seagull Monument on Salt Lake's Temple Square honors the bird that helped save Mormon pioneers' crops from crickets in 1848. *Author photo*.

The early Layton-Kaysville area apparently benefited from what may also have been a similar miraculous event. Grasshoppers, rather than the more famous Mormon crickets, caused the majority of the insect damage in pioneer Utah. (Crickets were hardly a nuisance in Utah after 1850.)

During the summer of 1854, grasshoppers threatened to destroy all the crops of settlers in the Layton-Kaysville area. This insect horde rose one morning like a low, dark cloud. However, huge wind gusts soon came from the eastern canyons and carried the grasshoppers out over the Great Salt Lake. Millions of dead insects later washed up on the shores of the lake, and most of the settlers' crops were spared.

While gusting canyon winds occasionally occur in winter, early spring or late fall, they are very unlikely to happen in the summer, according to northern Utah weather records. In fact, historically, this is one of only two recorded canyon wind gust events in the summer months for Davis County. From mid-May to late September, these winds have otherwise very rarely blown.

The same windy "miracle" was repeated at least twice, though in Salt Lake County. A year later, in 1855, in the western area of Salt Lake County, swarms of grasshoppers threatened settlers' crops. Once again, a providential wind came along and blew the insects into the Great Salt Lake.

The same thing happened again in 1868 in Salt Lake. After noticing the quantities of dead insects in the lake that year, Benjamin LeBaron wrote, "I consider this later deliverance from the grasshoppers just as great and miraculous as the former 1848 rescue from the ravages of the black crickets."

The years 1854–56, 1867–72 and 1876–79 are believed to have been the worst years of grasshopper infestations in northern Utah during the pioneer era.

BUFFALO ABOUNDED
IN 1820s UTAH

It is the plains of the Midwest that most people think of when roaming herds of bison come to mind. However, there is evidence that these large mammals once meandered in Utah, as far south as Kane County.

Karen D. Lupo, writing in *Utah Historical Quarterly* (Spring 1996), said her research showed that bison herds in prehistoric times were most concentrated in Utah, in the Willard Bay area.

The buffalo were hunted by Native peoples in Utah up to ten thousand years ago. Bison skeletons have been found in the High Uintas, Echo Canyon, Utah Valley, Parowan Canyon and along the shores of the Great Salt Lake and Utah Lake. Notwithstanding, there are few firsthand accounts of buffalo being killed in Utah. Even the Ute Indians were described as fish eaters and had no buffalo hides or fried meat.

Although Mormon pioneers found herds of bison so dense east of the Rocky Mountains that they had to have advance parties clear them out of the way, bison were not prevalent in Utah in 1847. An 1850 report by Mormons say a few buffalo were encountered in the Salt Lake Valley that year.

It may have been severe winter storms around and before 1845 that killed most of the buffalo in northern Utah. Even some Jim Bridger tales talk about deep snow wiping out the animals. The last bison in Utah Valley may have been killed by cold and snow in the winter of 1845.

Another Native American legend states that it was 1820 when a fierce winter storm wiped out many buffalo in Utah. Some Shoshone Indians

Bison abound on Antelope Island today, but they were transplanted there. Buffalo may have been all but wiped out in northern Utah as a result of severe winters in the early nineteenth century. *Author photo*.

to the north in the Snake River Valley also have oral traditions that claim buffalo were prevalent there until about 1824, when a massive winter storm all but wiped them out.

Still another possibility: according to Lipo's article, trappers and Native Americans may have used guns and horses to wipe out what bison were left in the area. Elias Adams, an early Layton, Utah settler, said in his history *Elias Adams: A Pioneer Profile*: "I can remember numerous buffalo skulls lying around in the hollow. They had starved during the hard winter before the pioneers came which was told about by the Indians."

Mountain man Osborne Russell, who kept a detailed journal of his nine years (1834–43) in the Rocky Mountains, mentioned herds of buffalo. Near Lava Hot Spring, Idaho, he reported, "Portneuf: here we found several large bands of Buffaloe."

Later, he said of that same southeast Idaho area:

> *In the year 1836 large bands of Buffaloe could be seen in almost every little Valley on the small branches of this Stream at this time the only traces which could be seen of them were the scattered bones of those that had been killed. Their trails which had been made in former years deeply indented in the earth were over grown with grass and weeds. The trappers often remarked to each other as they rode over these lonely plains that it was time for the White man to leave the mountains as Beaver and game had nearly disappeared.*

Later, Russell noted in Yellowstone, "Thousands of Buffaloe carelessly feeding in the green vales contribute to the wild and romantic Splendor of the Surrounding Scenery." He said about the Great Salt Lake area, "The Buffaloe have long since left the shores of these Lakes." He was also prophetic in predicting the demise of the bison, as he also stated in the appendix of his journal:

> *The vast numbers of these animals which once traversed such an extensive region in Nth. America are fast diminishing. The continual increasing demand for robes in the civilised world has already and is still contributing in no small degree to their destruction, whilst on the other hand the continual increase of wolves and other 4 footed enemies far exceeds that of the Buffaloe when these combined efforts for its destruction is taken into consideration, it will not be doubted for a moment that this noble race of animals, so useful in supplying the wants of man, will at no far distant period become extinct in North America. The Buffaloe is already a stranger, altho so numerous 10 years ago, in that part of the country which is drained by the sources of the Colorado, Bear and Snake Rivers and occupied by the Snake and Bonnack Indians.*

Still another tale in Box Elder County claims that a small herd of bison—the last one there—was wiped out by local Indians soon after white settlers entered the area.

Don Grayson, another bison researcher, concluded that buffalo were very prevalent in Utah until about seven hundred years ago. A climate change then reduced the growth of grasses as the mainstay of feed for the large animals. Thus, between climate change, harsh winters and nineteenth-century man's mass slaughters, the animal became endangered.

Locally, today, Antelope Island offers the best opportunity for observing these large animals. Farther north, Yellowstone National Park is also home to many bison.

Note that bison were not on Antelope Island when either the Mormon pioneers or government explorers were first on the isle. They were added in the early 1890s.

PART IV

UNFORGETTABLE
TRUE TALES

MULTIPLE VOLCANIC HOAXES IN UTAH

It was a Utah hoax of mountainous proportions. There was supposed to be a large volcano steaming in the north arm of the Great Salt Lake, northwest of Corinne, Box Elder County. That was the widespread word initially. But the *Salt Lake Tribune* of March 8, 1897, reported: "That volcano story. It is proved to be complete humbug. Nothing of the sort there."

A *Tribune* reporter went out to the remote area west of Corinne and found it to be false. No volcano, no earthquakes and no meteors were found. And no one interviewed had reliable testimony of such an occurrence.

This was not the last volcanic hoax in Utah. A *Salt Lake Telegram* headline on November 2, 1902, reported, "Live Volcano Reported in Beaver County in Southern Part of Utah." Dr. D.A. Turner of Milford, Beaver County, claimed that some earthquake disturbances were "probably due to eruption in Mt. Baldy," a peak more than twelve thousand feet high in the Tushar Mountains, east of Beaver.

Although it is true that there is evidence of ancient volcanic activity in that area, his conclusion was proven inaccurate. Still, there were claims from local residents of smoke and dust rising near the peak in the fall of 1902. It is apparently true that earthquakes did rattle the Beaver area that autumn. Puffer Lake's level was lowered by a quake that also increased the flow of the Beaver River. Some homes had dishes fall out of cupboards and windows broken during a quake a year earlier.

So, yes, there were likely earthquakes around Beaver in 1901–2, but no direct volcanic activity has happened there since prehistoric times.

SHAKEN BY EARTHQUAKE.

Severe Earthquake Wrecks Many Buildings.—Many Utah Towns Shaken Up.

Earthquake Increases Water.

Marysvale, Nov. 24.—Farmers on City creek and Baldwin creek, in Piute county, are hoping and praying that the results of the recent earthquake on those streams will be permanent. The volume of water now flowing in each of those streams is nearly twice what it was before the big shake. Users of water from City creek believe their increased flow was from Puffer's lake, and those using water from Bullion creek believe they are now receiving the water that before the earthquake ran down Fish creek, on Gold mountain, which has diminished in its flow since the earthquake.

Above: The north end of the Great Salt Lake was featured in a prank involving a volcano suddenly coming to life in 1897. *Author photo.*

Middle: "Shaken by Earthquake." Wasatch Wave, *November 15, 1901.*

Bottom: "Earthquake Increases Water." Salt Lake Tribune, *November 26, 1901.*

Another, more elaborate volcanic hoax came along later in Washington County, likely in the 1920s or 1930s. Southern Utah historian Bart Anderson of St. George sometime talks about this prank in his historical lectures. Although no exact date is known, it took place in an ancient volcano cinder cone located between Snow Canyon and Veyo.

Teenagers carried old tires or brush into the top of the volcano and then lit them on fire as a group of dignitaries were traveling by on Highway 18—or, in another version of the story, as local churchgoers were departing their meetings one Sunday. A few sticks of dynamite might have even been used for more special effects.

Either way, that fake eruption caused such excitement that some geologists were called in before it was determined to be a hoax. (It is worth noting that a search of old newspapers found no reports of this hoax.)

WHEN FRANKENSTEIN VISITED CLARKSTON

The rural Cache County community of Clarkston was the site of an ongoing prank in the 1940s. According to a story on Ancestry.com, Clarkston had its own version of Mary Shelley's iconic monster with a Frankenstein masquerade.

Essentially, Dennis Griffin, a young teenager at the time, ordered through the mail an elaborate rubber Frankenstein mask. He and friends would take turns in the evening darkness putting the mask on and frightening people walking alone. The boys were wise enough to perceive that frightening groups was somewhat dangerous, since too many unpredictable things could happen.

These "sightings" sparked both excitement and fear in the community. One time, Griffin was chased by a policeman and rushed home, slipped through his bedroom window and pretended to be asleep. Griffin and friends wore just the mask and had regular clothes on otherwise.

At one point in the 1940s, some youths were so afraid of the monster appearing that they would not attend the Church of Jesus Christ of Latter-day Saints' MIA (youth) activities at night for a time. Local leaders did receive complaints of the monster sightings, but Griffin's recollection was that most knew it was youths looking for a quick scare.

The neighboring town of Newton also heard of the monster, and some were afraid it would appear there, too.

Griffin remembers wearing the mask about four times. He eventually loaned it to friends and then to other, older boys. One of those boys never

Above: Clarkston is located in Cache County, northwest of Logan. It is also near the Idaho border and was the scene of a Frankenstein tale in the 1940s. *Author photo*.

Left: A 1935 promotional photo of Boris Karloff from *The Bride of Frankenstein*, in which he played Frankenstein's monster. *Public domain, Wikicommons*.

returned the mask, and Griffin failed to ever get it back. Where it went is a mystery.

He recalls that some sightings continued into the late 1940s and perhaps the early 1950s—with or without a mask. Some of the pranksters may have been copycats. Still, Griffin recalls that this pranking lightened a bit of the mood during World War II and through concerns about nuclear war afterward. In a small, dull farming town, the sightings simply sparked a little excitement, he noted.

Surprisingly, a detailed search of Cache Valley newspapers in the 1940s and 1950s revealed not a single mention of this Frankenstein. Perhaps no one wanted to encourage an escalation of the sightings. But the Newton Town Library has a detailed account of this prank written by Griffin.

SOUTH WEBER'S ECCLESIASTICAL DISPUTE

Why is South Weber located in Davis County, when its very name is synonymous with neighboring Weber County? Why is it that about one-fourth of what some still consider Hooper territory is not in Weber County but in Davis County?

The answer to both of these perplexing identity queries relates to a significant county boundary change made in 1855. South Weber was indeed originally in Weber County. Why it jumped counties is an ecclesiastical tale as much as it was a government decision. According to Utah historian Glen M. Leonard in the book *A History of Davis County*, an ecclesiastical disagreement resulted in the boundary of Davis County moving about one mile north of where it was originally established.

President Brigham Young visited the South Weber area in October 1853 and declared that a fort should be established there. Kington Fort, named after the area's first bishop of the Church of Jesus Christ of Latter-day Saints, Thomas Kington (his name is misspelled "Kingston" in many other histories), was then created. A listing in the March 8, 1855 *Deseret News* lists South Weber as being in Weber County, more proof the community switched counties.

However, soon Kington and Lorin Farr, the Weber LDS Church Stake president in Ogden, had some sort of serious disagreement, though what it was about was never recorded. (Leonard suspects it might have simply been a boundary-related issue.) Lee D. Bell, author of *South Weber*, called the dispute "a falling out" in his history of the community. He believes the fact

Above: The town of South
Weber (*top half of photograph*)
is now in Davis County.
It originally resided in
Weber County, before
an ecclesiastical dispute.
Whitney Arave photograph.

Left: Lorin Farr, circa
1890. *By C.R. Savage. Public
domain; courtesy Church History
Collections, the Church of Jesus
Christ of Latter-day Saints and
Intellectual Reserves Inc.*

that the Utah territorial legislators intervened in the argument proves how serious a disagreement it must have been.

The book *East of Antelope Island* simply mentions that "there was some difference between President Farr and Bishop Kington, so it [South Weber] was annexed to Davis County by the (territorial) legislature."

Territorial legislators in 1855 redefined the Davis-Weber county line due to prompting from Kington. (Perhaps he was one of the state's first lobbyists?) The legislature moved the Davis County line northward. This essentially put Kington's ward in Davis County and meant that President Farr no longer had any jurisdiction over his congregation. They were under Davis County's stake president.

The county line was moved south to the Weber River at the east end of Davis County. This meant that the Weber town of Uintah (previously called East Weber) was created to define what settlement remained on the north side of the Weber River.

The new Davis County town had already favored the name South Weber, even though it was now in a different county, but at least it was indeed on the south side of the Weber River.

Now, jump ahead to 1877, when a related boundary change was made. Perhaps someone looked at a map of Davis or Weber County and saw the unusual zag in the county line created in the 1855 change. This time, instead of keeping the twist south in Davis County's border beyond South Weber, the county line out west was now moved north about a mile to parallel the change made twenty-two years earlier in the South Weber section. This now made the Davis-Weber boundary line fairly straight from where it left the Weber River until it reached the marshes of the Great Salt Lake.

Besides a crooked boundary, another factor in favor of moving more Weber County land into Davis County—by moving the Davis line northward on its west side—was that Davis County was clearly still the state's smallest county. Legislators in 1877 may have felt the tiny county could use a little more land.

The most significant effect of this related boundary change was that Hooper, originally known as Muskrat Springs and established in 1852, was now split. This created South Hooper on the Davis County side. It was originally huge, going all the way south to today's 1700 South Street (Antelope Drive) before the days of a West Point, Clinton and Syracuse. Over the decades, as those three cities were established, South Hooper shrank dramatically and only the section of unincorporated Davis County there was left.

This sign in Davis County denotes the unincorporated and unofficial portion of Hooper, attributable to boundary changes in the community's earliest years. *Author photo.*

The South Hooper name also faded, as the rural area stretched only from West Point at about 5000 West Street and State Road 37 ("Pig Corner") about a mile north to the county line. But today some of these rural residents still consider themselves Hooperites, even though they reside in a different county. A "Welcome to Hooper" sign is still posted in a field along Highway 37, deep into Davis County's Hooper. New delivery drivers are likely baffled and lost by the abrupt address changes when they cross from the Weber County Hooper to the Davis County side.

Eventually, West Point may annex all of this remaining Davis County Hooper, as it is the only community that likely could.

UTAH'S FIRST BASKETBALL
TEAM WAS ALL WOMEN

What are the beginnings of college and prep basketball in Utah? They aren't likely what you might think. But the University of Utah women's basketball team has a legendary heritage, though it's obscure and intermittent.

Utah collegiate women not only started hoop play in the Beehive State in the late 1800s but also likely played some of the first public hoops—if not the first-ever such games—in the western United States.

"University Basket-Ball. Girls Defeat the Boys in the First Open Game" was a May 16, 1897 headline in the *Salt Lake Tribune*. The story reported that in the premiere game played on the new outdoor field at the University of Utah, the women's squad beat the men's team by a score of 8–6.

The women started timidly in the game but soon took command, according to the story. The field was reported to be too dusty and soft "for pleasurable playing," though it had now been improved. The new playing field was on the north side of the campus and shaded by large willow trees in the afternoon.

The first report on women's basketball in the *Deseret News* was likely printed on January 19, 1900, when the Lowell school girls' team soundly defeated the girls of Salt Lake High School (forerunner to West High School), 16–2.

Apparently, boys didn't think basketball was a manly enough sport in the early years. For example, back when BYU was Brigham Young Academy (before 1903), only women played hoops there. A photograph in the *Encyclopedia of Mormonism* in the sports entry shows the women's team that

the notable colleges and girls' schools the country, but its introduction in t Lake is comparatively recent. The M. C. A. ladies had practiced but a rt time when, early in last January, game was instituted at the University of Utah. Something of an innovation at first, it is now established as ideal of physical exercise, and ten ing ladies in this institution of learn- dodge and throw the basket-ball th enthusiasm and skill which in- e for all time the popularity of the ne in Salt Lake. Verily, the enthusi- n of the college girl is irresistible. d the result will be—what? More ms, interschool and intercollegiate tests, and above all, a type of lthy, graceful womanhood. coff at this latter assertion, you who p on the masculine tendency of the l-of-the-century girl, with your cant rases of "usurpation of man's pre- atives" and the like, but go. just e if you may, and see the University ls play basket-ball. Bright eyes, wing cheeks, supple forms, quick ions, unerring movements and fear- ness. These are the things you will l characterizing every one of the And ask them what they think of game. If one or all of them speak

Capt. Miss Hewell

Capt. Miss Hyde

The Basket Ball Teams of the University of Utah.

The University of Utah is well known in the twenty-first century for its elite men's football program. But in the late nineteenth century, its women's basketball ("Basketeers") team made history. One of the nation's first women's basketball teams, they even defeated the men's team in 1897. Salt Lake Tribune. *April, 18, 1897, page 9.*

won the Brigham Young championship in 1900. The coach was a man, and there were seven female players, all clad in long dresses.

The women of early basketball in Utah played wearing very long and baggy dresses. An illustration in the April 18, 1897 *Salt Lake Tribune* shows the University of Utah girls' team wearing similar long dresses. That story referred to "basket-ball" as a "mild rival of football" and said that Utah State College in Logan, as well as Rowland Hall, the Mutual Improvement League (an LDS Church–sponsored team) and the YWCA had all organized girls' hoops teams.

Several months later, a June 4, 1897 *Tribune* report on "basket-ball" included drawings of girls at the University of Utah and showed more streamlined dresses (but still very loose fitting) that went only to the knees. That report also said that a public game by the University of Utah and league teams was the "first contest of the kind ever played west of Chicago."

The University of Utah women's team won that game, 8–3, over the Mutual Improvement League. Jean Hyde, captain and center of the U of U team, led all scorers with four points. There was some controversy in the game when Miss Hafen of the Mutual team tried to talk to one of the umpires about so many uncalled fouls on the opposing team. (The game featured two umpires and a referee.) She was warned that to do so again would result in a foul. (Strangely, the drawing of the referee showed him carrying a long stick.) The coach of the U of U team was Elmer Qualtrough.

A *Salt Lake Herald* story of May 17, 1897, credited Miss Lucile Hewitt as being the U of U student who petitioned the Athletic Association at the school to let her women's team play, with coeducation being a key concept in the early years of basketball teams. That same story mentioned that one player had sustained a broken nose during play, though the story characterized the game as "exercise, simple and pure, vigorous and real."

Privacy of women's basketball was also a key early concern, at least for prep play. "Basket-Ball Maidens. The Elusive Sphere Chased behind Closed Doors" was a November 6, 1897 headline in the *Salt Lake Tribune*. The story said that the front doors of the market, where the Salt Lake High junior girls practiced, were locked so that no males would see them play. A sign on the door stated, "No spectators allowed," so that "their gyrations should not be observed by any odious males." (The girls' team did have a male coach, though.)

Sadly, women's competitive basketball play didn't last long in the early years of the twentieth century, partially because boys' play soon became popular and pushed the girls aside. It was also likely that in that era, some felt it inappropriate for girls and women to be playing so competitively. However, many decades later, with the advent of Title IX in the late 1970s, girls' and women's basketball teams in both high school and college eventually returned in force.

WHEN BYU BANNED FOOTBALL

"Opposed to the Game of Football" was a headline in the *Deseret News* on December 8, 1905. Too many injuries and even the death of a Utah player in a game during the 1900 season combined to create a ban on football at the Provo school.

Football was played at Brigham Young University, when it was named Brigham Young Academy, from 1896 to 1903. At about the same time as the Brigham Young University name came along in 1903, the sport of football was discontinued there for some sixteen years.

In fact, "Mormon Church Is against Football," was a November 18, 1908 headline in the *Salt Lake Tribune*. This report stated that all schools operated by the Church of Jesus Christ of Latter-day Saints would now also ban football. The matter had been under review for a year, and many students petitioned for football, but it was considered too violent and led to too many injuries.

This wasn't just an LDS Church stand against football. Institutions all over the United States, like Harvard and Columbia, were also against the sport for its brutality. "Not for gentlemen" was a common saying at schools that banned football. "Football is a hospital feeder" was another slogan against gridiron play.

Nationwide, at least forty-five deaths and hundreds of serious injuries were reported in the 1905 college football season. President Theodore Roosevelt that year met with sports officials from Harvard, Yale and Princeton in an attempt to get football injuries reduced. President Roosevelt's sons played the game. He wasn't out to halt the sport, just to make it safer.

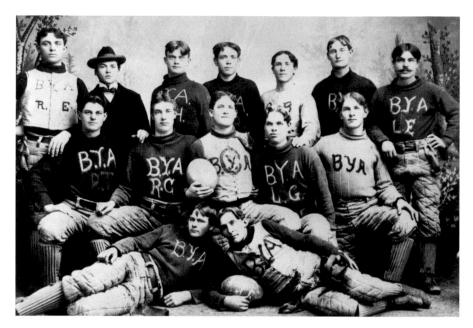

The Brigham Young Academy football team in 1897. (The Academy was the forerunner school to Brigham Young University.) BYU banned football in 1903 for sixteen years for being too violent. *Utah State Historical Society.*

"Present Football Is Too Dangerous" was a November 19, 1909 *Salt Lake Tribune* headline. Schools in New York State banned all football games in 1909, citing the fact that "bones were broken and pupils otherwise injured." By 1910, the University of Kansas also banned football. Some football rules had been changed in the early 1900s to try to make it safer, but numerous injuries continued.

The Utah state legislature saw House Bill 165 proposed in 1909. It would halt all football play in the state, especially at the University of Utah and the Agricultural College in Logan. However, the bill was withdrawn before a vote.

In BYU's case, it was the General Board of Education of the LDS Church that prompted the ban on football. According to the *Deseret News*, some students left BYU or didn't attend because of this ban. (Of course, no one dreamed back then that BYU would ever be the national champion in college football, as it was in 1984, some sixty-four years after the ban was lifted.)

As football was banned at BYU during those years, a churchwide ban meant the sport was also halted at Weber Stake Academy (forerunner of Weber State University). Finally, more rule changes and advances in equipment helped make the game safer for players.

Football returned to BYU in 1919 as an intramural sport. The next two seasons, BYU had limited college play. The Cougars finally had a full football season in 1922, though the team's record was a dismal 1-5.

Football was perhaps its most brutal in the late nineteenth century. The *Ogden Standard-Examiner* reported in 1885 on the Ogden High football team. "The boys have laid in a good supply of shin plaster, and for a week or past, they have had a carpenter busily engaged in manufacturing crutches. Several competent surgeons have been retained for the occasion [upcoming game] and will be in attendance."

It wasn't just brutality that cancelled football games in the early twentieth century. An October 3, 1908 game pitting the University of Utah's freshman team against Ogden High was cancelled due to bad weather. A few years later, a soggy field also led to a cancellation. A November 1907 gridiron contest between West High School and Ogden High was cancelled by the board of education due to rowdy public disturbances caused by Salt Lake players in their improper advertising of the upcoming game.

Finally, college teams routinely played high school teams in Utah in the early twentieth century. In October 1912, the University of Utah freshmen whipped Ogden High, 56–0. With a shortage of other prep teams in the area back then, preps played college teams as far away as Montana.

WHEN BASEBALL DISRUPTED LDS GENERAL CONFERENCE

On the evening of Saturday, October 4, 1930, in the middle of a General Priesthood meeting talk by the Church of Jesus Christ of Latter-day Saints' president Heber J. Grant, the wrong flip of a KSL Radio studio switch caused havoc.

The network radio feed of the World Series instantly replaced President Grant over the Tabernacle sound system, going to some six thousand priesthood holders. The startling baseball broadcast continued for eight minutes while Sylvester Q. Cannon, presiding bishop of the Church, raced from the Tabernacle to KSL to get the problem fixed.

In those days, KSL was located atop the Deseret News Building (the former Union Pacific Building) on the southwest corner of Main Street and South Temple. That was about a half block from the Tabernacle.

KSL Radio head engineer John Dehnel confirmed that the incident is not folklore. It did take place. Records are spotty on the event, though. Some historical articles have only briefly mentioned the event and have erroneously stated that it happened in the 1920s during General Conference. There's a lack of information on the incident because KSL Radio was embarrassed by it. For some reason, neither the *Deseret News* nor the *Salt Lake Tribune* reported on the mishap afterward.

Dehnel had some of the only information on the event. He believes KSL was using special speakers on Main Street to broadcast the World Series to the public when, somehow, that alternate feed accidentally got switched into the Tabernacle. It had to have happened during General Priesthood session,

The Salt Lake Tabernacle hosted thousands of church meetings before the new Conference Center opened. In a 1930 meeting, a World Series broadcast accidentally disrupted proceedings there. *Author photo*.

because Dehnel said that's the only time when KSL would have been airing something different than General Conference. (The first World Series action, between the St. Louis Cardinals and the Philadelphia Athletics, to air instead of a priesthood meeting involved a close steal of second base. Philadelphia ended up winning the World Series, four games to two.)

Dehnel said KSL's limited records also indicate that church leaders were quite amused by the accident. The oldest living General Authority (at the time this was originally researched), Elder David B. Haight, ninety-two, of the Quorum of the Twelve, was living in Berkeley, California, in 1930 and said he didn't personally hear the General Priesthood meeting. Still, he had heard about the incident and acknowledged that it really happened. However, he stressed it was a mistake.

Ironically, President Grant's opening General Conference address on Friday, October 3, 1930, had lauded the advent of modern technology. He made reference to how amazing it was that several church members in New Zealand had written him recently about hearing KSL loud and clear. Also, Grant had made the first broadcast on AM-1160 eight years earlier, on May 6, 1922.

The first LDS Conference radio broadcast had taken place just six years earlier, in October 1924, just two years after **KSL** (named **KZN** for its first eighteen months) originated.

Although the "World Series" General Conference incident happened during radio's early years, a mini-disruption of General Conference happened almost ninety-one years later. KSL-FM Radio listeners to General Conference on Saturday morning, April 3, 2021, were interrupted by about ten seconds of rock music that accidentally cut into the broadcast. The author and a Utah radio enthusiast both heard the interruption. It seems that technical glitches can still happen in modern times. The glitch sounded like music from sister station **KRSP-FM**.

WHEN SIR HILLARY INVADED THE HIGH UINTAS

There's a legend that Sir Edmund Hillary, one of the first two men to conquer Mount Everest, in 1953, also climbed Kings Peak in Utah.

This is actually a true story, but it happened in the summer of 1978, when Sears and Kellwood (an outdoor equipment manufacturer) was testing camping gear in the Yellowstone drainage of the High Uintas.

Hillary, then age fifty-nine, was said to have had little trouble hiking Kings Peak and the Uintas. No stranger to Utah, Hillary had also floated the Green River in 1969 as part of the centennial commemoration of John Wesley Powell's 1869 exploration of the area. Hillary had first visited the High Uintas in July 1962, when he and his family enjoyed a four-day camping trip in the Granddaddy Basin area. "New Zealand Mountain Climber and Family Thrilled with Pack Trip into High Uintas Areas" was a July 19, 1962 headline in the *Uinta Basin Standard*.

Duchesne District ranger Larry Colton served as a guide for the Hillarys as the family hiked and fished. According to the newspaper, Hillary's wife, Lady Louise, and their three children—Peter (seven), Sarah (five) and Belinda (three)—ventured into the primitive area of the High Uintas. Hillary was under contract with the U.S. Forest Service to make a report on campgrounds in the western United States that year.

The family began at Mirror Lake, backpacked into the Granddaddy Basin area and then returned to Mirror Lake. They did a lot of hiking, but

Bald Mountain from Mirror Lake in Utah's High Uintas, where Sir Edmund Hillary visited on several occasions. *Author photo*.

A section of the High Uintas, southwest of Bald Mountain. Sir Edmund Hillary hiked and camped in the High Uintas in 1962 and 1978. *Author photo*.

not on any serious peaks. Hillary said this trip was for finding "smiling" and not "fierce" peaks, according to the newspaper account.

The only negative to the trip were all the mosquitoes they encountered, but they said they got used to them. Another Utah newspaper, the *Vernal Express*, reported that on that 1962 trip, Hillary declared it "absolutely wonderful."

RATTLESNAKES TO MUMMIES IN MANTI

The town of Manti in central Utah has bizarre stories of both rattlesnakes and mummies.

According to www.ldschurchtemples.com, "The Manti Utah Temple was built on a rattlesnake-infested site, known as the Manti Stone Quarry." The Temple's construction started in 1877 and was completed eleven years later, in 1888, as the third Temple in Utah. Located on "Temple Hill," the material for the exterior of the structure was obtained from quarries in the hill where it is located.

This hill was apparently rattlesnake heaven. Not dozens, but hundreds of the venomous reptiles called it home when the first pioneer settlers arrived there. In fact, according to *Ensign* magazine of March 1978, settlers "battled rattlesnakes for possession of the valley."

According to several pioneer diaries referenced on scholarsarchive.byu.edu, the Temple Hill had the greatest infestation of all.

The first pioneers arrived in the fall of 1849 and sought winter refuge by building dugouts on the south side of the hill that would later be known as Temple Hill. After what was one of the worst winters in the area (according to local Native Americans), a warming spring brought hope to the settlers. But as temperatures warmed in the spring of 1850, rattlesnakes began to appear everywhere on the hillside, even in people's dugouts, beds and other places.

One pioneer diary claimed that 300 snakes were killed during the first night they appeared. Another stated that at least 500 were killed. Still another

The Manti Temple sits on a prominent hill in Manti, where rattlesnakes once dominated and where tales abound of caverns and tunnels in the rock underneath. *Author photo.*

claimed that 1,500 were wiped out. The extermination of the reptiles continued for several more nights. Settlers primarily used torches and clubs to kill the snakes. Miraculously, there was not one report of a snakebite.

According to Utah Pioneer Stories on Sanpete.com, the spring of 1850 brought the following development: "Soon hundreds of hissing rattlesnakes appeared in the dugouts. They were everywhere! As the sun began to go down the snakes became more plentiful and the battle was on. The settlers armed themselves with clubs, torches and anything else that they could use as a weapon against hundreds of snakes."

Some twenty-seven years later, in 1877, presumably most of the snakes were gone, as Brigham Young announced the Temple site. President Young reportedly said, "Here is the spot where the Prophet Moroni stood and dedicated this piece of land for a Temple site, and that is the reason why the location is made here, and we can't move it from this spot; and if you and I are the only persons that come here at high noon today, we will dedicate this ground" (*LDS Church News*, March 8, 1958).

Some now question if Moroni actually dedicated the site for this Temple. That's because the story relies on a single source and the occurrence was never included in any official Manti Temple histories, such as its dedication proceedings.

Mormon pioneer settlers spent their first winter in Manti (1849–50) hunkered down in this rocky hill, where the Temple now stands. *Author photo*.

Construction began that same year. The first step was to level out the hilltop so a Temple could sit there. It required significant blasting, as the hill contained a lot of rock. In fact, even today, Temple Hill has dirt that extends downward only from a few inches to several feet before hitting all rock.

When the Temple builders were creating the western foundation for the structure, they discovered an extensive network of caves and tunnels. This is where the rattlesnakes nested in winter several decades earlier.

Rattlesnakes have left a lasting impression on the Manti area. Indeed, one of the tallest mountain summits in the area is named Rattlesnake Peak (8,612 feet above sea level).

There are also other, more fanciful tales regarding the Manti Temple. There are unconfirmed stories of strange inscriptions on some of the rocks found inside Temple Hill's caves during the early construction. Other tales speak of metal plates and mummies found beneath the hill in its caves. Some stories claim that local Native Americans spoke about an ancient temple and altar being on the hill long ago. These Indians also warned of the dangers of going inside any of the caves. A guaranteed true tale of Manti is that you used to be able to drive through the Manti Temple.

The original construction included an arched tunnel at ground level, just wide enough for a small automobile or wagon to pass through. The archway was filled in decades later and is now a large window surrounded by a stone wall. People used to joke that Manti was the only Temple you could go through without a church-issued recommend.

Another ironic fact related to the construction of the Manti Temple is that much of its lumber came from the Hell's Kitchen area of a nearby forest.

GOLD MINE LEGENDS IN TAYLOR CANYON

L egends of gold mines are some of the most intriguing tales in the American West. Ogden has its own storied fables. Perhaps the two (yes, at least two) lost gold mines in Taylor Canyon top the list.

Taylor Canyon, located east of Ogden's Twenty-Seventh Street and a popular hiking gateway to Malan's Peak and Malan's Basin, may actually contain some lost gold mines.

According to the *Ogden Standard-Examiner* of June 26, 1913, "Gold Exposed by Bolt of Lightning" in Taylor Canyon. The story states that an unnamed prospector was traversing the canyon on June 23 that year when a bolt of lightning "shattered the cliff and revealed the rich metal, but in haste to get out of the storm the miner gained insufficient identification marks." He reportedly was still hunting for the spot, but with no further updates over the years, he apparently never found the treasured spot again.

The *Salt Lake Tribune* of October 18, 1959, had a story titled "Ogden's Lost Mine. Taylor Canyon Holds the Secret of a Mine Abandoned Nearly 50 Years." This story describes a different gold mine in the canyon, abandoned in 1911, that a man by the last name McDonald had created. He also built a nearby cabin that the story reported had been found a few years later by a group of boys. The boys said they saw a nearby shaft that went twenty-five feet or so into the mountain. That structure was destroyed by vandals in 1917, and Union Pacific, which later owned and managed Taylor Canyon for its timber, apparently collapsed the mine for safety reasons. Many years later, McDonald returned with his two sons, but they were unable to find the mine.

The mouth of Taylor Canyon, east of Ogden, is home to fanciful stories of lost gold mines. *Author photo.*

Was the mine really a gold mine? The *Tribune* story stated:

> *When a miner is just prospecting, he usually pitches a tent or makes a lean-to for his shelter. This is all he needs, for he is just hunting ore—he'll be moving on soon, if he doesn't have any luck. But when a miner discovers good ore and plenty of it and he plans on staying on the spot, then, and not until then, does he build a cabin—especially as fine a cabin as Mac's cabin was.*

There was a separate, more modern cabin also located in Taylor Canyon, between the trail switchbacks on the south slope. That cabin's origin is its own mystery. Taylor Canyon has an extensive mining legacy. The *Standard-Examiner* of October 6, 1899, reported a working gold and silver mine in the canyon called the "Last Chance Tunnel." J.H. Haines was the miner of this claim, which ran 175 feet into the north side of Taylor Canyon.

The *Standard* of August 31, 1904, stated that there were ten known mining claims in Taylor Canyon. Among the names given to these mines are Excelsior, Curb Stone, Ogden Salmon, Psyche, Merrymack and Maybeso.

Many mines in Taylor Canyon had names and were publicly known. One big question is why no claim was filed for the McDonald gold mine. There may be lost mines in Taylor Canyon, but none gained widespread fame like the La Plata silver mine northeast of Ogden. Why? Perhaps because they weren't very profitable.

There are stories and legends of other mines in the Ogden area, particularly those around Willard Peak and Ben Lomond Peak.

THE DARK SIDE
OF LAGOON PARK

There is one taboo subject at all amusement parks: fatalities and accidents. But accidents do happen. Nothing in life is totally safe.

However, rest assured that, statistically, you are far more likely to be injured or killed in a car accident on the way to or from Lagoon Amusement Park in Farmington, Utah, than on any of the park's many rides and attractions. Lagoon is Utah's and the Mountain West's oldest and largest amusement park.

Lagoon has likely averaged about 1 million visitors a season during the past three or so decades. With just three ride fatalities from 1960 to 2021 (using a half million annual visitors as average before 1980 and one million a season thereafter), the odds of being killed on a Lagoon ride would pan out at many millions to three against dying on a ride.

With only twenty-seven known fatalities in the park's long history dating to 1886, that isn't a bad safety record at all. The park would prefer to have had no deaths. But it can clearly be concluded that most of the ride-related deaths at Lagoon were caused by a patron's own negligence or recklessness. In some accidents, riders "tested" their safety restraints or even tried to exit the ride on their own.

Three of the fatalities on rides—the most of all—are from the wooden Roller Coaster. Add a worker's death on the coaster's tracks, and that's four fatalities related to the Roller Coaster, making it the park's most dangerous ride.

Left: Lagoon Park in Farmington, Utah, has totaled at least twenty-five fatalities in its long history dating back to 1886. *Author photo*.

Right: The wooden Roller Coaster has historically been the most dangerous ride at Lagoon. It is also one of the park's oldest, having opened in 1921. *Author photo*.

Swimming and diving produced Lagoon's most fatalities in its early years. In fact, the *Ogden Standard-Examiner* on July 29, 1912, stated in an editorial that due to all the drownings at Lagoon, its lake should be only three feet deep. It also stressed that more warnings for riders of Lagoon's Scenic Railway ride should be posted, given its turbulent nature.

What follows is a listing of all of Lagoon's known mishaps. The list does not claim to be a complete history of all accidents at Lagoon. Still, it is likely the most comprehensive list available anywhere.

DEATHS

Henry John Barnes, fifty, of Farmington, drowned in about three feet of water at Lagoon's Lake on August 3, 1907. According to the *Deseret Evening News* of August 5, 1907, he had been drinking and was believed to be intoxicated. His body was not found until the next morning.

A swimmer poses before making a perilous-looking dive into the Lagoon Swimming Pool on July 24, 1923. The diving board appears to be about thirty-six feet high. A line of men behind are awaiting their turn. The pool was the site of eight fatalities over the decades, almost one-third of all fatal accidents in the park. *Courtesy of Utah State Historical Society.*

Herbert Lee Reeder, nineteen, of Ogden, drowned in Lagoon Lake on June 5, 1909. He was a passenger in a shell-like boat with a friend, Fred Naisbitt. The boat capsized when the two were changing oars. Reeder, who could not swim, sank to the bottom, and Naisbitt nearly lost his own life trying to save him. Others came from shore and tried to help. The June 6, 1909 *Ogden Standard-Examiner* article on the accident noted that Lagoon management has made no effort to patrol the lake in order to keep it safer.

"Emma Youngquist Drowned at Lagoon." The young woman was boating on Lagoon Lake with a boyfriend on July 28, 1912, when she decided to change places and row the boat. The young man disagreed with that action, but she stood up anyway, the boat rocked and both fell out. The young woman drowned, her body being found twenty-five minutes later, sixteen feet from shore and in eight feet of water (*Davis County Clipper*, August 2, 1912).

Three riders and one park worker have been killed by the Roller Coaster ride at Lagoon, with the most recent fatality occurring in 1989. *Author photo*.

"Railroad Man Is Killed at Lagoon." Albert Fulton, twenty-seven, a Denver & Rio Grande Railroad employee, died at Lagoon on July 15, 1914, when he struck his head on the bottom of the pool and fractured his skull. Fulton leaped from the Lagoon high dive and hit the water perpendicularly, as he was believed to have slipped off the platform. The depth of the pool water was clearly posted at six feet (*Ogden Standard-Examiner*, July 16, 1914).

"Earl E. Logston Killed after Races." Logston, of Salt Lake City, was killed on the Lagoon racetrack on September 5, 1921, in a vehicle accident. He and a companion were trying to see how fast they could drive around the track following the day's official races there. Somehow, a light in the car came loose, stuck in the steering gear and caused the car to crash into a fence. A splintered rail struck Logston and instantly killed him (*Davis County Clipper*, September 9, 1921).

"Auto Racer at Lagoon Killed." Chris Chioles, twenty-three, died when the race car he was in crashed into a fence around the Lagoon racetrack on July 24, 1922. (Chioles was the vehicle's mechanic.) Charles W. Herman, of Salt Lake City, was driving the vehicle and was injured in the crash. It is believed that a cloud of dust on the track had blocked Herman's vision (*Ogden Standard-Examiner*, July 25, 1922).

"Husband Dies after Saving Wife in Flood." Arnold Christensen, thirty-eight, a Lagoon employee, rescued his wife from floodwaters that struck Lagoon on August 14, 1923, after a cloudburst in Farmington Canyon. Farmington Creek was overflowing and caused thousands of dollars in damage to the park. Christensen, a brother of A.C. Christensen, the Lagoon Park manager, "died of heart disease, caused by excitement and exertion," according to reports. He and his family were living in a tent at Lagoon that summer. This is undoubtedly the strangest of all deaths in Lagoon's long history (*Salt Lake Tribune*, August 14, 1923).

"Ogden Man Killed on Dipper at Lagoon." George Burt, nineteen, of Ogden was killed instantly on Saturday, July 26, 1924, when he fell twenty-five feet from the Dipper roller coaster (today's wooden Roller Coaster). Burt was making his fourth ride of the night and insisted on standing up during the ride. He eventually lost his balance, slipped out and hung onto the car but was dragged thirty feet down one incline and partially up another before he lost his grip and suffered the fatal fall. He had a broken neck (*Davis County Clipper*, August 1, 1924). The coaster at the time likely did not have seat belts.

The Roller Coaster is one of Lagoon's most thrilling attractions, because the wooden construction makes the ride seem old and rickety. *Author photo*.

"Park City Miner Meets Death at Lagoon July 4." Tobias Oritz, a Park City miner formerly from Santa Fe, New Mexico, died in the Lagoon Swimming Pool on the afternoon of July 4, 1925. He leaped from the pool's high dive and struck his head on the bottom. He was under the water ten minutes before he was located and pulled out. Resuscitation was used unsuccessfully. His neck was not broken, so it is believed that he was stunned under water and drowned. "This is the second accident of the kind that has occurred there since the diving place has been in use." A similar death from diving happened earlier, although no details are available (*Davis County Clipper*, July 10, 1925).

"Rocking Boat Brings Death to Young Boy." Henry Wright, fifteen, of Salt Lake City, drowned when horseplay on a boat while fishing on Lagoon Lake knocked him into the water (*Weekly Reflex*, June 30, 1927).

"Park City Woman Accidentally Killed at Lagoon." Mrs. Luka La Fay Goodfellow, of Park City, died instantly from an accident in the Lagoon Fun House on July 13, 1930. She was accidentally thrown from the "fun wheel" in the Fun House and struck her head against a post. (This was the original Fun House, which burned down in the 1950s, not the later version.) (*Davis County Clipper*, July 18, 1930).

Ernest Howe, twenty-one, of Ogden, stood up on the Roller Coaster ride and fell out as it made its first turn. He died on impact with a fractured skull on August 20, 1934 (*Salt Lake Telegram*, August 21, 1934).

Samuel George Marler, twenty, of Idaho Falls, Idaho, died on August 17, 1942, from a neck fracture three days after diving into the Lagoon Swimming Pool (*Weekly Reflex*, August 20, 1942, and *Salt Lake Telegram*, August 18, 1942).

James Young Hess, twenty-three, of Farmington, died from injuries sustained from being struck by a Roller Coaster car at Lagoon on September 1, 1946. Hess was hit by the car while working on the ride's scaffolding. He suffered skull, leg and arm fractures and died at a Salt Lake hospital (*Salt Lake Telegram*, September 2, 1946).

F. Dana Loveless, fifty-one, of Salt Lake City, was found drowned in the Lagoon Swimming Pool by workers. Foul play was not suspected (*Salt Lake Telegram*, August 5, 1952).

Michael Scott Johnson, seven, of Granger, drowned in the Lagoon Swimming Pool on August 1, 1961. The boy had gone to the pool with his mother and three sisters. The mother told the boy to wait for them by the women's dressing room, but he reportedly responded, "I'm no sissy." When the rest of his family came out of the dressing room, the boy could not be found. He was discovered moments later floating lifelessly under the surface in five feet of water. He had not learned to swim (*Salt Lake Tribune*, August 2, 1961).

William Stewart, twenty-three, of Layton drowned in the Lagoon Swimming Pool on July 5, 1975. He was found at the bottom of the pool's deep end and could not be revived (*Herald Journal*, July 7, 1975).

Ryan Beckstead, six, of Bountiful, was killed on the Puff the Little Fire Dragon ride at Lagoon on April 30, 1989. This mini children's Roller Coaster did not malfunction. The ride operator hastily decided to give the riders a second ride and failed to notice that Beckstead, in the rear car, was already almost out of his seat, believing the ride to be over. Beckstead was tossed out of the ride and stuck between the tracks. No one, including his father, could reach him before the coaster came back around a second time and struck him on the tracks, killing him (*Deseret News*, May 1, 1989). Lagoon subsequently enhanced the restraints on this ride to hopefully prevent any such future accidents.

Kilee King, thirteen, of Bountiful, died on July 9, 1989, after she fell thirty-five feet from the lead car of the Roller Coaster. She suffered a broken neck and had been trying to "get air" by pushing her legs against the seat of the car as it went over a hill. The result was that she was thrown out of

Lagoon's Wild Mouse is one of its wildest rides. However, it is pure folklore that this ride, or any of its previous versions, had any cars crash to the ground. *Author photo*.

the ride's car. Her lap bar had remained closed but failed to keep her inside the car (*Deseret News*, June 13, 1989). Soon after, Lagoon moved all of the coaster seats permanently slightly forward to lessen the chances of this type of accident happening in the future.

A thirty-two-year-old man died several days later from critical injuries suffered in a fifty-foot fall from the Sky Ride on August 14, 2021. (The Sky Ride is a tram ride, virtually identical to ski lifts, that transports riders from one end of Lagoon to the other.) The ride has no seat belts, but the man had to have purposely climbed out of his seat in order to fall. Videos taken by other riders showed the man with two arms hanging onto one of the front enclosure bars and his feet dangling. He eventually lost his grip and fell to the ground. The Sky Ride opened at Lagoon in 1974 and had never suffered any significant accidents. Unlike any other ride at Lagoon, this tram ride (like all such "lifts") is subject to strict governmental regulations and regular inspections. There was no malfunction here, as the man willingly left the safety of his seat and ultimately caused his own death. Was it a suicide attempt, or a stunt gone wrong? The truth may never be known.

There have been at least six other non-attraction-related deaths at Lagoon since 1978.

Neil Keith Hansen, twenty-eight, of American Fork, died in a rodeo accident at Lagoon on July 3, 1978. He was thrown off a bull he was riding. The bull then kicked him fatally (*American Fork Citizen*, July 13, 1978).

Park officials say one person died in the park from a seizure and another from a heart attack.

A Lagoon employee, Denise Davis, sixteen, was critically injured on June 29, 1981, after she fell off a garbage truck in the parking lot. She died a few days later. Another person drowned in the old Lagoon Swimming Pool after illegally entering the park grounds after hours.

An Idaho girl was killed when she was struck by a car in the Lagoon parking lot on May 16, 1996.

A seventy-two-year-old Roy man died from a heart attack at Lagoon on May 17, 2003. A lawsuit later claimed that the man did not receive prompt enough emergency care (*Deseret News*, June 11, 1989, and August 1, 2004; *Provo Daily Herald*, May 20, 1996).

Others likely died of illnesses and other natural causes at Lagoon over the years, especially before 1980.

The Fire Dragon metal roller coaster at Lagoon has an impressive safety record. Its lone major accident happened to an employee in 1983. *Author photo*.

SOME NONFATAL ACCIDENTS AT LAGOON

July 5, 1898: The young daughter of Dr. J. Thomas of Salt Lake City suffered moderate burns to her chest from a large fireworks rocket that went haywire and exploded near her during a pyrotechnic display at Lagoon (*Salt Lake Herald*, July 6, 1896).

June 16, 1900: Andrew Jenson, a ZCMI employee, rescued two young women from drowning in Lagoon's lake. He was walking over a bridge on the lake and heard cries for help. With a loud musical presentation going on at Lagoon at the time, it was hard to hear. He supposed the women had been flung from an overturned boat. He was the only person nearby at the time (*Salt Lake Herald*, June 20, 1900).

Early April 1906: Charles Boylin of Farmington, who looked after the grounds and animals at Lagoon, was seriously bitten by a monkey. He suffered a paralysis to both arms initially but, after several weeks, recovered full use of his limbs (*Box Elder News*, April 19, 1906).

April 22, 1907: Two painters suffered serious injuries when their scaffold fell to the ground after the ropes broke. They had been painting the roof of the Lagoon Dance Hall, which had been replaced after high winds blew it off the previous fall (*Deseret News*, April 23, 1907).

July 18, 1902: "Accident at Lagoon. Reckless Man Causes Injury to Several Children" read a July 19, 1902 headline in the *Salt Lake Herald Republican*. An unknown man with a palm tree fan in his hand struck the horse that powered the Merry-Go-Round ride at Lagoon to make it go faster. As a result, Sarah Jane Cameron, fourteen, was knocked down and out of her seat and was stepped on by the horse. She sustained bruises and cuts. Hattie Crabbe, twelve, was knocked off the ride and hit the picket fence surrounding the ride. She was badly bruised. An Ogden boy was thought to have a broken arm from the accident, but it was only a sprain. The man who caused the accident disappeared into the crowd and was not found.

May 30, 1908: Undoubtedly Lagoon's most disastrous opening day, with two injuries, one serious. Logan Balderston of Bountiful was seriously injured on Lagoon's scenic railway when he was thrown out of the car on a turn and fell forty feet to the ground. He broke his leg, his ribs were displaced and his heart was moved a few inches. Doctors initially thought he would not survive, but he gradually improved.

Leonel Layton, of Layton, broke his arm on the park's skating rink (*Davis County Clipper*, June 5, 1908)

April 28, 1908: Lorin H. Heninger of Ogden was seriously injured at Lagoon while riding "bumping the bumps," a type of early park ride. No other information is available. The ride may have been similar to today's dodge 'em car rides (*Davis County Clipper*, August 28, 1908).

July 4, 1915: "M.L. Rose Seriously Injured at Lagoon." Rose, a Lagoon employee, was struck by a scenic railway car in the park. The force of the crash pushed him six feet and to the ground. He had four broken ribs and had to have a damaged kidney removed (*Weekly Reflex*, July 8, 1915).

July 24, 1922: Charles W. Herman, of Salt Lake, an auto racer, suffered a concussion, cuts and bruises when a race car he was driving crashed into a fence around the Lagoon Race Track. (Chris Chioles, twenty-three, of Salt Lake City, his mechanic, was also in the vehicle and died in the crash.)

August 16, 1924: "Three Injured When Lagoon Balloon Bursts." Three men were hurt, two seriously, when a gas balloon being readied to go airborne to advertise Lagoon exploded, causing burns to workers (*Weekly Reflex*, August 21, 1924).

July 14, 1930: Edward Miller, twenty-two, from Pennsylvania, suffered lacerations of the head and a fractured elbow after diving from the high dive at the Lagoon Swimming Pool (*Weekly Reflex*, July 17, 1930).

August 30, 1951: "Train Victim, 5, 'poor' in Hospital." Karen Winter, five, of San Leandro, California, suffered a skull fracture, shock and body, head and leg injuries when she stepped into the path of the miniature train at Lagoon. The train was entering the depot and was traveling about five miles per hour and was unable to stop. The train had to be turned on its side of remove the injured girl. She had wandered away from her parents just before the accident (*Salt Lake Telegram*, August 31, 1951).

November 13, 1953: At 10:56 p.m., Lagoon's sixty-seven-year lucky streak of no fires ran out. It was a blaze! A Farmington resident, Fred D. Fellow, first noticed the fire. The skies were red and smoking. The flames were so high—up to three hundred feet—that they could be seen from twenty miles away in western Salt Lake City.

Owner Peter Freed was at his Sixteenth Avenue home in Salt Lake City. A neighbor who worked at the *Salt Lake Tribune* called to tell him of the fire.

Flames swept down the west side of the midway, destroying everything in their path. The front (east) end of the wooden Roller Coaster was wiped out. The Lagoon Fun House and the Dancing Pavilion were reduced to rubble. Also destroyed were the Tunnel of Horrors, the Shooting Gallery, a café, a taproom, several storehouses and small concession booths. The historic Merry-Go-Round was saved by a constant flow of water sprayed on it. Volunteer firemen from the city battled the blaze for more than six hours. No injuries were reported from the fire.

Looking at photographs taken by the *Deseret News* the morning after the fire, the scene looking out from the Merry-Go-Round resembled the aftermath of a nuclear explosion. Twisted metal columns were sticking out of the ground.

It was simply amazing that the east section of the Roller Coaster was almost totally destroyed and the Merry-Go-Round was spared. Thousands of spectators from Salt Lake to Ogden came to see the fire, which caused an estimated $500,000 in damages. The fire was undoubtedly the largest commercial blaze in Davis County in the twentieth century.

Lagoon had been closed since Labor Day for the season, though a few employees had stayed on for maintenance work.

The exact cause of the fire was never determined. It was suspected that an electrical transformer near the Lagoon Fun House had caused the fire. Spontaneous combustion and some greasy rags near the Fun House were also a possibility.

Even before the flames died down, the Freed family, owners of the park, had vowed to rebuild Lagoon. The park had insurance, but it didn't cover enough of the damage, as the entire west end and the ballroom were destroyed.

This was still a summer enterprise and one that had yet to make a profit. Only the Freeds' other business enterprises, the Freed Finance Company and a ranching business, kept them going.

Like a phoenix, Lagoon rose from the ashes and never looked back. It was eventually rebuilt bigger than ever.

July 29, 1954: "Gay Lagoon Coaster Ride Injures Eight." A train returning to the station on Lagoon's wooden Roller Coaster failed to come to a stop and crashed into another coaster car being loaded. Injuries to the neck, back and a fractured pelvis were among the worst of the injuries. Other persons were bruised. The ride operator saw the errant coaster car coming and moved the outgoing car around the bend, a move that, with emergency brake application, probably lessened the injuries (*Ogden Standard-Examiner*, July 30, 1954).

September 2, 1954: Hans Gregerson, the nineteen-month-old son of Clyde Gregerson of Bountiful, suffered a fractured skull and other injuries when he fell backward and into the concrete water channel on the baby boats ride. The miniature tugboat ride then ran over the top of the boy, and he became tangled in the boat's propellers (*Deseret News*, September 9, 1954).

June 23, 1958: Carolyn Brain, fifteen, of Salt Lake City, lost the end of a little finger when it became caught in a flange on the side of a slide at the Lagoon Swimming Pool.

Circa mid-1960s: According to a March 2016 Facebook post by Laurie Capener of Layton, she was a teen waiting in line for a ride near the original Wild Mouse (then located at the north end of the midway). She said she saw the Wild Mouse malfunction: "Watched one car not make it up the last hill, while another one rammed the stalled car from behind. Several kids were injured. I would never get on it again."

Apparently no one was seriously injured, but this accident may be the source of overblown urban legends that the Wild Mouse jumped off the tracks and some riders were killed.

June 27, 1967: "Ride at Lagoon Hurts Worker." The *Salt Lake Tribune* reported on June 28 that a Lagoon employee, Greg Wilson, sixteen, of Salt Lake City, was seriously hurt when a midway car at an attraction struck him from behind.

April 20, 1968: Danny Smith, twelve, of Bountiful, was critically injured when he fell from a playground swing at Lagoon and the swing struck him in the head. The accident happened when the park was not open (*Salt Lake Tribune*, April 21, 1968).

June 27, 1968: Six riders were treated for injuries and released after an arm of the Octopus ride fell to the ground. One of the main pivot pins on the ride sheared off, causing the crash. No one was seriously hurt. This ride was taken out of Lagoon for good soon after.

May 31, 1976: "Fall at Lagoon Hurts Employee." The *Ogden Standard-Examiner* stated on May 31 that James Holt, seventeen, of South Weber, a Lagoon employee, was in fair condition after a fifteen-foot fall at the park. Holt had climbed up on the Jet Star ride to dislodge a stuck car on the tracks when he fell after the car moved. He suffered a broken back and pelvis.

September 7, 1980: "Guard OK after Attack by Caribou at Lagoon." Steve Keller, twenty-two, of Layton, a Lagoon security guard, was attacked and bruised by a loose caribou at the park. The area was off limits to Lagoon visitors. The animal was later sedated with a dart gun and put back in its enclosure (*Lakeside Review*, September 11, 1980).

June 11, 1983: A Lagoon employee, Shauna B. Lassen of Clearfield, lost her left arm after it was severed by the Fire Dragon ride as it raced by.

June 20, 1983: Bart Page, sixteen, of Centerville, a teenage worker at Lagoon, lost his right foot when it became caught in the control mechanism

Opposite, top: The Tilt-a-Whirl ride is one of Lagoon's oldest rides. An employee was seriously injured operating the ride in 1983. *Author photo.*

Opposite, bottom: The Helicopters is a popular children's ride at Lagoon. However, an accident on the ride in 1984 injured two riders. *Author photo.*

Above: The Jet Star II is one of Lagoon's most turbulent rides. Accidents on this ride produced injuries in both 1987 and 2002. *Author photo.*

for the Tilt-a-Whirl ride. Page somehow pushed his foot through a narrow slot, where it was crushed (*Provo Daily Herald*, June 21, 1983).

1984: Two children were injured when the Helicopters ride plunged to the ground. A lawsuit followed.

1987: A Pittsburgh, Pennsylvania woman said she was injured on the Jet Star II ride when it came to an abrupt halt. Also in 1987, a Ketchum, Idaho man said he was hurt when a Jet Star II car struck his car from behind.

June 19, 1989: "Bad Wire Shocks Lagoon Visitors, One Employee." A faulty wire at a coin-operated basketball game at Lagoon caused a minor electrical shock to four patrons and one park employee. The short circuit sent 110 volts of electricity into a metal fence behind the game, where the five people were shocked (*Provo Daily Herald*, June 20, 1989).

1990s: A young girl suffered a serious ankle injury when the Sky Ride struck her as she exited the attraction. She required multiple surgeries to repair a torn Achilles tendon. She reportedly received more than $100,000 in a settlement from a lawsuit.

June 10, 1991: A two-by-six-foot cross board on the Lagoon Roller Coaster came loose and broke the arm of an Elko, Nevada man, Frank Greco, eighteen. He was riding at the time, and it struck him from overhead as the coaster car went by.

August 1996: A sixteen-year-old Centerville girl working at Lagoon was bit in the arm by a cougar at the Lagoon Zoo. The animal was euthanized later to determine if it had rabies or other diseases.

July 3, 2000: A Layton man injured a finger and his arm in the Drop water slide at Lagoon-A-Beach.

September 2000: A South Jordan man injured his knee after crashing into the end of the pool of the Drop ride in Lagoon-A-Beach's waterslide area. (This was at least the third injury that resulted in a lawsuit against Lagoon regarding the Drop slide.)

August 9, 2001: A freak accident on the Scamper, a children's bumper car ride, frightened but did not hurt a male rider, age six. A pole at the top of one of the ride's cars shorted out, produced an arc of electricity and causing a heavy piece of metal about one and a half inches long to heat up and fall onto the seat next to the boy.

Summer of 2002: Jessica Jackson was riding the Jet Star II with her mother, aunt and cousin. The brakes on the incoming car behind them malfunctioned, and that car struck their car. She and most of her group suffered minor injuries from the crash,

2012: An elderly man shattered his leg in a fall getting off the Dracula's Castle ride. He apparently could not exit the ride quickly enough before the next car came around the corner and bumped him to the ground.

CRIMINAL BEHAVIOR:
SHOOTINGS AND ROBBERIES AT LAGOON

"Shooting at Lagoon. Bartender Alexander Has Encounter with Thieves. They Wanted Free Beer." In just its second year at its current location, Lagoon had a shootout at its saloon. As quoted in the *Salt Lake Tribune* of June 17, 1897, Alexander "ordered them to throw up their hands, but they fired six shots at him instead—It was dark and their aim was poor—One bullet out of the six fired at him took effect, lodging in his arm—Will not be able to mix drinks for a few days to come." The men ran away after the shooting.

"Sixteen-Year-Old Boy Arrested for Trying to Wreck Lagoon Train." Charles Fowler of Salt Lake was arrested after it was determined that he had tried three times to derail the miniature train at Lagoon in 1903. He placed obstructions on the train tracks (*Salt Lake Herald*, August 26, 1903).

"Jimmie Johns Is Shot by Officers." On July 15, 1916, police had to arrest twenty men for disorderly conduct at Lagoon's Dance Hall. Johns was shot four times during the incident (*Journal* [Logan, UT], July 18, 1960).

Lagoon has had some very weird happenings over the decades. How about a foreign spy and a bomb plot? "Dancing Master Proves to Be Spy; Man Who Taught Dancing at the Lagoon Tried to Blow Up Pavilion on Soldiers' Day," was the headline in the September 7, 1917 *Davis County Clipper*. "The professor who had been teaching dancing at Lagoon has turned out to be a German spy," that article stated.

The bomb didn't go off. If it had, dozens could have been killed or injured.

It was reported that the professor disappeared but was later captured and held in the prisoner's camp at Fort Douglas. The newspaper stated that rumors were circulating that the spy had already been convicted and executed. The article reported that another German, who had been living with a family in Centerville, had also been arrested as a spy and sent to Fort Douglas.

"Man Arrested for Beating Up Girl at Lagoon May 30." Blanche Price, of Salt Lake City, was beaten up and robbed by Roy Thomas, nineteen, of Salt Lake City, on May 30, 1930. He attacked her in the parking lot, stole an automobile and fled to Ely, Nevada. He was arrested after he returned to Salt Lake (*Weekly Reflex*, June 5, 1930).

"Four Arrested for Burglary." Four teenagers from out of state were arrested at Lagoon on November 18, 1934, for trying to smash open penny arcade machines. The youths caused an estimated $1,000 in damages to twenty-five arcade machines. They also smashed doors, tables and cash registers (*Salt Lake Telegram*, November 20, 1934).

"Thugs Bind Guard, Get Lagoon Cash." Two experienced criminals escaped with up to $5,000 after they bound and gagged a night watchman in the Lagoon office at about 4:00 a.m. on June 5, 1950. The masked robbers took all the cash they could find, including pennies. They were never caught (*Ogden Standard-Examiner*, June 5, 1950).

"Davis Nabs Two Juveniles on Wounding of Woman." Two boys, ages twelve and thirteen, were shooting a .22 caliber rifle about two blocks east of Lagoon. One of their wild shots struck Janice Coombs Hansen, nineteen, of Salt Lake City, in the left shoulder while she was standing north of the Lagoon Swimming Pool (*Salt Lake Tribune*, May 22, 1951).

"Shots Fail to Stop Youths after Lagoon Car Crash." A Farmington deputy marshal fired four shots at two sixteen-year-old youths at Lagoon on August 9, 1951, after they raced away after striking another car in the Lagoon parking lot. The two teenagers had tried to enter Lagoon without paying and then began their run. Their car stalled in Farmington Canyon, and they were arrested walking back to town. The same two youths had been referred to juvenile court a week earlier for public intoxication at Lagoon (*Salt Lake Tribune*, August 28, 1951).

July 15, 1959: "Lagoon Worker Hurt in Fracas." The *Salt Lake Tribune* of July 17 reported that Dale Thurston, nineteen, of Farmington, an amusement park worker, suffered a deep cut on his forearm during an altercation at the park. Two men from Salt Lake and a woman were arrested as part of the violent stabbing incident.

"2 Salt Lakers Jailed after Shooting." Two Salt Lake men were involved in a shooting in front of the Lagoon Dance Hall on August 2, 1961 (*Salt Lake Tribune*, August 3, 1961).

June 15, 1991: Three teenage boys were stabbed during a fight at Lagoon. This was not gang related.

Malfunctions occasionally happen on Lagoon rides, usually causing only delays and inconvenience.

July 24, 1999: The Skyscraper ride malfunctioned, and its brakes temporarily stopped working. The ride continued about an extra twenty-five minutes before it was finally stopped. Some passengers loved the extra-long ride with a view; others felt trapped. There were no injuries.

July 1, 2002: The Roll-o-Plane ride malfunctioned and left eight passengers stranded on the ride for thirty minutes. No one was injured.

October 14, 2002: The Samurai ride broke and left twenty-eight riders trapped in the cold and in an upright position for one hour and forty-five minutes.

PART V

TALES OF THE BRINY GREAT SALT LAKE

WHAT'S UNDER THE GREAT SALT LAKE?

W hat's in the Great Salt Lake? What riches and mysteries do its briny waters contain?

The lake, its islands and surrounding environs have been the subjects of study by scientists, environmentalists and those seeking recreational opportunities. The lake water itself is thick, literally, with salt, and the history of the huge inland sea is thick, too, with fact and legend. Its natural contents are largely unique, because the lake is unique—five to six times saltier than the oceans, with no outlet. It is so huge that it influences the weather for hundreds of miles. Its waters are mined like the earth for salt and minerals, and its one natural life-form, brine shrimp, are harvested like farm crops.

Under its surface are the wrecks of an unknown number of aircraft, train car parts and sandbars. And beneath its bed are oil, layers of salt-encrusted minerals and fetid masses of pickled sewage.

While the lake is inhospitable to some boaters, swimmers at lakeside resorts have been fascinated by its ability to keep them floating "like corks." In more recent years, the lake has been shrinking in times of drought, and more of its former bottom than ever is exposed.

The constantly changing lake has a colorful history and has inspired a number of tall tales about monsters who may call its depths home. Don Currey, a University of Utah geography professor, says that visiting Antelope Island is a metaphysical experience. "You're surrounded by buffalo and antelope. You're walking through time. It is the archetypal basin and range. You're riding high. You have a sense of being in the middle of great basin tectonics. It's a class in itself."

Amid a drought, the dry lake bed of the Great Salt Lake appears barren, except for a tumbleweed. However, there are still things hidden below the briny lake's diminishing waters. *Author photo*.

True to its name, the lake water holds plenty of salt. Concentrations of salt in the lake vary considerably from season to season, from year to year and in different locations and depths, but it is generally five to six times saltier than the ocean.

Wallace Gwynn, a saline geologist with the Utah Geological Survey, said the Union Pacific railroad's earthen-fill causeway across the north end of the lake has divided it into two parts. The area north of the causeway is more salty than ever, while the south is less salty. He said this man-made barrier has lessened the dramatic "float like a cork" phenomenon that was so strong on the lake's south end at Saltair Resort earlier in the twentieth century.

Mineral extraction is a big business, with Great Salt Lake Chemicals Corporation employing huge evaporation ponds and a trench near Little Mountain, west of Ogden. Smaller companies, such as Trace Chemicals Company in West Haven, Weber County, also capitalize on the brine's mineral contents. Other companies harvest salt for the table, cattle or winter roadway use from the lake.

The salt water in the lake itself is usually too concentrated to freeze. However, during calm winter weather, fresh water from streams flowing into

Saltair Resort, circa 1880–1920. *Photo by George Edward Anderson. Public domain, L. Tom Perry Special Collections, Harold B. Lee Library, Brigham Young University.*

the lake can freeze before it mixes with the lake water. Rain or snow also doesn't instantly mix with the brine. At times, there may be a narrow layer of fresher water on top of the lake. It takes wind and some action within the lake to mix the waters.

This has sometimes caused an ice sheet several inches thick to extend from the Weber River west to Fremont Island. In the early 1900s, this ice sheet made it possible for coyotes to cross to Fremont Island and attack sheep pastured there.

The breakup of thick ice has also been known to form icebergs. One iceberg in 1942 was thirty feet high and one hundred feet wide. Icebergs also formed in 1984 during the wet winter when the lake's salinity dropped. The scene was described as mountains of shaved ice that roamed the lake acting like bulldozers, pushing aside anything in their way—trees, fences, old cars.

It's no secret that fish occasionally float into the Great Salt Lake from its tributaries, like the Weber or Bear Rivers. However, they are usually already dead.

History books refer to various attempts to stock the lake with eels, oysters, crabs and the like, but none has succeeded. Most sea life can't survive

An old glass bottle sits in sand, under what used to be many feet of briny water in the Great Salt Lake, before the lake began to recede. *Author photo.*

the extremely salty waters, and those that can are not able to stand the wide temperature changes of the lake water from winter to summer. But freshwater fish, like carp, were reported in the flooded lands of Centerville and Farmington around the lake in 1984. Carp have always been found near places where fresh water flows into the lake, such as at Ogden Bay.

During the wet years of 1983–85, the lake's southern waters were only about two and a half times brinier than the ocean because of the influx of so much freshwater. According to Steve Phillips, media coordinator for the Utah Division of Wildlife Resources, there was a potpourri of fish—white bass, trout, catfish and others—in the lake during the mid-1980s around the Jordan, Weber and Bear River drainages.

Phillips said the fish would get flushed into the lake. They survived for several years until the salinity began rising. He doubts that any remain in the lake today, although some carp may survive in areas of Farmington Bay.

The lake's only regular resident sea life are the brine shrimp. The brine shrimp's transparent body is rarely more than a half inch long. They are used as fish food in aquariums, and the Great Salt Lake supplies 90 percent of the world's inventory of brine shrimp eggs. Hat Island is the shrimp's favorite spot.

One study estimated that as many as 25 brine flies per square inch, or 370 million per beach mile, can be found along the lake during their warm-weather peak.

In the mid-1970s, one study found that the lake is part of the flyway between Canada and Mexico and that as many as 250,000 ducks and 10,000 Canadian geese may be born annually on the lake and its shores. More pelicans may be born on the lake's islands than anywhere else in the nation.

WHEN A LAKEMOBILE
ROAMED THE GSL

Like its larger cousin, Antelope Island to the north, Fremont Island isn't always truly an isle at all. A huge natural sandbar during low lake levels can offer dry-land access to the somewhat mysterious, privately owned "island."

The community of Hooper, directly east of Fremont Island, was ripe with tales of a man from West Point who, years earlier, when the Great Salt Lake was at very low levels, used to drive a special truck all the way to Fremont Island over only six or so inches of water.

His name was Charles Stoddard. He leased Fremont Island in 1932 and began ranching sheep there. Not wanting to rely completely on boat travel, Stoddard put caterpillar-like chains on the rear wheels of a Model A Ford truck and created what others called a "Lakemobile" to access Fremont Island for several decades.

This natural sandbar, which Stoddard first discovered, was large but not straight. So, during the low lake levels of the early 1930s, he put upright railroad ties along the shallowest part of the sandbar, from west of Syracuse— some ten miles—to Fremont Island to mark its course. Then, as the lake level rose, he had what David E. Miller in *Desert* magazine of May 1949 referred to as a "Salt Lake Trail on the Desert" to follow.

So, Stoddard basically drove a truck in the middle of the Great Salt Lake! His only major problem was an ice floe that struck his truck in March 1942. Although the lake's briny waters do not freeze easily, the incoming fresh river water can, and thus a small iceberg hit his truck and knocked it on its side.

Charles Stoddard of West Point, Utah, prepares his legendary "Lakemobile" for travel through the Great Salt Lake in November 1942. Stoddard used the vehicle to access Fremont Island and his ranching herds by way of a natural sandbar—in only eighteen inches of water. However, a large, floating sheet of ice struck the Lakemobile in March 1942 and carried it a mile southward, trapping it in a bog of near quicksand at this location. Stoddard returned eight months later and got the vehicle moving again. *Courtesy of Utah State Historical Society.*

The Fremont Sandbar today is mostly dry, because of the shrinking Great Salt Lake. This view is from the Antelope Island Causeway toward Fremont Island. *Author photo.*

Stoddard managed to upright the truck and get the ice away, but the Lakemobile ended up in a bog and wasn't freed until more than eight months later, in the following November. Even then, he had to replace the truck's salty motor oil and spark plugs and use kerosene to loosen the cylinders. The old truck started up and moved again.

Stoddard was also known to use a small boat, mounted on a two-wheeled trailer and pulled by a team of horses, to access the island. He even told Miller that some youths once rode bicycles to the sland, while riders on horseback and even a touring car had successfully made the trip as well.

By the early 1940s, the sandbar was briefly but almost completely above water late one summer season. So, instead of having to boat sheep to and from the island, Stoddard was able to herd them on mostly dry ground. Only the south end of the sandbar was then underwater, just a few inches deep. By 1948, the GSL had risen two feet in seven years, and Stoddard had to travel by boat in his remaining years of ranching.

Twenty years later, in the late 1960s, travelers on the newly built dirt road causeway to Antelope Island could see two black posts and a gate sticking up in the water. That marked Stoddard's "road," the sandbar. In the summer of 1979, the briny water around those black posts was not only four feet deep but also very muddy. The Great Salt Lake continued to rise for another seven years.

Because of drought and water diversion, those posts were eventually removed. A swath of rocks by the Antelope Island Causeway marked the sandbar path to Fremont Island. By then, the sandbar was almost always above water each late summer.

36

QUICKSAND AND OTHER
BOTTOMLESS GSL STORIES

It has always seemed like quicksand in the Great Salt Lake was nothing more than a fanciful myth. However, according to the *Ogden Standard-Examiner* of May 28, 1939, two horses actually died in such "non-existent" quicksand. "Horses Die in Quicksand of Great Salt Lake after Driver Missed Stakes Marking Route. Ogdenite Is Haunted by Experience as Steeds Drown," was the headline. Mike Boam of Ogden was driving a light rig powered by horses traveling to Fremont Island over the then-underwater sandbar. This route was often used in the 1930s to travel to the 2,943-acre Fremont Isle.

Boam said that without warning his two horses "stepped into a patch of quicksand," and "several hours of labor failed to extricate the animals." He had to wade about five miles through knee-deep brine along the "salty highway" to reach the mainland. When he reached his home in Ogden, he was exhausted but could not sleep. "The look in the eyes of those horses when I left them wouldn't let me rest," he told the *Standard-Examiner*. By the following day, both horses were dead, "victims of their own exertions and the brine they had drunk to quench their thirsts."

Quicksand is simply sand inundated with water under circumstances in which the liquid can't escape. While the animals didn't sink out of sight, they were trapped in a sticky mess.

Also, in 2020, the Diesel Brothers, who used to own Fremont Island (before they sold it to a nonprofit group; that group then donated it to the State of Utah), reported in a YouTube video that some of their tractors

A closeup of the rocky jetty that marks the beginning of the seven-mile-long sandbar to Fremont Island. *Author photo.*

and equipment had become stuck in "quicksand" along the Fremont Island sandbar. They were finally able to remove them with great difficulty. They described the briny sand as "peanut butter mud."

Sadly, there are other horror stories for horses involving Fremont Island. There were wild ponies living on the isle until the late 1980s. An Associated Press story of March 22, 1988, states that the Idaho rancher who was leasing the island at the time shot them because the cost of removing all of them was prohibitive and they were overgrazing on the isle. He intended to put sheep there. He was able to capture and remove about one hundred of the ponies by barge, but the remaining forty were too hard to catch.

A private pilot flying over the island had spotted the carcasses. The Welsh ponies were placed on Fremont Island in the late 1950s as part of a failed plan to make a recreational development on the island. The animals soon became wild.

Horses and sheep weren't the only animals to inhabit Fremont Island. For more than two weeks in the mid-1940s, a "phantom" coyote escaped extinction from hunters. The animal, which was believed to have hitchhiked

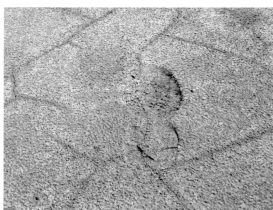

Above: The Great Salt Lake lake bed, even when above the regular water level, can produce its own sticky version of quicksand, akin to peanut butter, when wet. Fremont Island sits in the background of this picture of the adjoining sandbar. *Author photo.*

Left: Once the lake bed of the Great Salt Lake dries out, it equals just a slight amount of sinkage, as these footprints prove. *Author photo.*

to the isle on a rare chunk of iceberg in the Great Salt Lake, had killed some fifteen of the eight hundred sheep grazing there. An army of dogs and twenty armed men failed to kill the coyote during multiple attempts.

"Phantom of Isle Still Eludes Dogs" and "Phantom Coyote Has Hunters Marooned in Lake" were two headlines in the *Standard-Examiner* from March 26 and March 29, 1944, respectively.

High winds caused the dogs to lose the scent of the coyote and prevented the hunters from leaving Fremont. "Hunters Again Foiled in Phantom

Coyote Chase; New Expedition Scheduled," stated the March 31, 1944 *Standard-Examiner*. Hunters joked about needing to use a silver bullet to stop the animal, as numerous regular bullets had proven ineffective.

Finally, on the fifteenth day of the hunt, the hunters had success. "Island Coyote Killed in Lake Waters," was the headline on April 4 in the *Salt Lake Tribune*. A bullet had finally wounded the coyote. It jumped in the lake and tried to swim away. A speedboat caught up to it, and it was hauled aboard and killed.

Four other coyotes had been speedily killed on Fremont Island in 1942 after they had killed numerous sheep, but none were as elusive as the phantom coyote.

The most famous part of Fremont Island is the historic cross that Kit Carson carved on the north end on September 9, 1843. Only about six inches long, this Christian relic was left during the first government survey of the Great Salt Lake and island. Writings of the exploration prove that Carson made the cross, though uncertainty about its origin swirled into the early 1940s. "New Speculation Arises about Island Cross," stated the November 2, 1943 *Standard-Examiner*. This story questioned the cross's origin and speculated that a bored sheepherder in the 1850s had created it. But soon after it was universally accepted that Carson was indeed the author of the cross.

A Salt Lake grave robber, John Baptiste, was exiled to Fremont Island in 1862 by Brigham Young for his crimes. However, he eventually disappeared from the isle and was never heard from again.

WHEN NO ANTELOPE ROAMED ANTELOPE ISLAND

Antelope Island is by far the largest and most popular isle in the Great Salt Lake. With Utah State Park status, the island is visited by thousands annually. However, is the island technically misnamed?

"Island Offers Nature Study. Antelopes Refused to Remain. Bathing Beaches Unsurpassed," was a July 2, 1922 headline in the *Salt Lake Telegram* for a story by Harvey Hancock.

The isle was originally named Church Island, because the Church of Jesus Christ of Latter-day Saints originally owned it and early pioneers vacationed there. The *Telegram* story states, "The name 'Antelope Island' became the name in common use after an attempt was made to range a herd of antelope placed upon its hills. The conditions were suited to these animals and their efforts to escape is one of the most tragic stories of animal life."

The dissatisfied leader of the antelope herd jumped into the briny waters and was willing to try to swim up to sixteen miles to the enticing green fields of the mainland of Davis County. The other antelope followed. Only one antelope reached the shore and died from exhaustion. The others drowned in the lake.

This extinction apparently happened some years before 1922. Soon after, a herd of buffalo was placed on the island. They flourished and did not attempt to flee the isle. In fact, the *Davis County Clipper* of September 12, 1924, stated, "for the last thirty years, the name Buffalo Island has been used interchangeable with the other two names [Church and Antelope]," because one of the nation's largest surviving herds of buffalo resides there.

Black Rock and Antelope Island, circa 1891. *Photo by C.R. Savage. Public domain; courtesy Church History Collections, the Church of Jesus Christ of Latter-day Saints and Intellectual Reserve Inc.*

Notwithstanding, it must be mentioned that some of the earliest pioneer visitors to the Island reported seeing a herd of antelope there.

The *Davis County Clipper* of November 17, 1933, reported, "Late in the fall of 1848 while riding at the north end of the Island, Lot Smith, Fielding Garr and Heber P. Kimball came unexpectedly upon a herd of antelope." Heber P. Kimball was a son of Heber C. Kimball, prominent LDS Church pioneer leader.

Thus, antelope may have naturally lived on the island in the mid-nineteenth century. Perhaps they were hunted out. Later, some antelope transplanted there but hated the conditions. There may still be some antelope living on the isle today, but buffalo far outnumber them. Buffalo Island, instead of Antelope Island, could have become its official moniker.

Antelope Island has also at times not been an island at all. "To Island by Land. Trip Can Be Made Practically Dry Shod. Road of Salt and Sand," was a September 24, 1900 headline in the *Salt Lake Tribune*. The story continued: "Great Salt Lake has been known as the 'Dead Sea of America.' If it is not dead, it certainly gives every evidence of being in the throes of dissolution." The story stated that there was nothing but four miles of glistening salt between what used to be the eastern shoreline of the lake and Antelope Island. A *Tribune* representative made the trip to the island by wagon and horses in thirty-five minutes "without urging the horses to any great extent."

Motorists on Antelope Island have to watch for buffalo. However, the isle's namesake animal, antelope, has a rare history there. *Author photo.*

One man told the *Tribune* that he wagered he could travel by land from the ranch house on the south end of Antelope Island to Saltair Resort, ten miles away, "with perfect safety."

Cattle were reported as doing well on Antelope Island. Not much wheat has been raised there due to extra-dry conditions. Farther north, the water conditions of the Great Salt Lake were reported as more favorable. Still, the hunks of decaying boats and other wreckage along the former lake bed were reported as not being very inviting in appearance.

EARLY SHIPWRECKS ON THE BRINY GSL

There seems to have been plenty of boaters on the Great Salt Lake in Utah's earliest decades who shipwrecked, or nearly so. A significant number of them ended up stranded temporarily on Fremont or Antelope Islands.

Perhaps the lack of weather forecasting, sparse communication and underestimation of the punch of the lake's briny-laden waves contributed to the disasters.

The first of these involves two near-wrecks by the lake's first known white explorers, the John C. Frémont party, which included mountain man Kit Carson, who conducted a U.S. government survey there. On September 9, 1843, Frémont and four of his men paddled a poorly made inflatable rubber boat to Fremont Island. However, halfway there, a strong wind began to blow, and whitecaps appeared on the lake's surface. They had great difficulty in reaching the isle, especially as air in the boat leaked out.

After their survey, they returned to the mainland but faced an even larger incoming storm. Carson's diary stated that they had not gone more than a league when an incoming storm threatened them and the boat was leaking air. Frémont urged them to "pull for their lives," Carson noted, and that "if we did not reach shore before the storm, we would surely all perish." Pulling at the oars with all their might, they barely made it. "Within an hour, the waters had risen eight or ten feet," Carson wrote.

Christopher Layton, a prominent early pioneer, is the namesake for today's Layton City. One of Layton's lesser-known experiences was a shipwreck in the Great Salt Lake. In April 1872, a small steamship, the *Kate Connor*, owned by Layton, ran ashore off Antelope Island (then known as Church Island) and became stranded.

The *Salt Lake Tribune* reported on May 2, 1872, that the accident happened during a big storm. There were about ten people onboard the craft, which was carrying cedar posts at the time.

The fierce spring storm almost swamped the boat, and the passengers scurried to safety on Antelope Island. Eventually, a sailboat was used to transport them back to the mainland.

Next, the wrecks get personal for the author of this book. A large pioneer map of the Hooper area on the wall at the Hooper City offices (drawn and produced by the late Hooper historian John M. Belnap) lists Nelson Arave, a great-grandfather of the author and the first Arave, as having wrecked a

This hand-drawn map by John M. Belnap, a late Hooper, Utah historian, highlights some early shipwrecks on Fremont Island, including one by the author's great-grandfather. *Author photo.*

boat on Fremont Island in the Great Salt Lake in 1874. Three years later, in 1877, there's a reference in the Latter-day Saints' *Millennial Star* (Vol. 39, p. 223) that states that Nelson Arave had built two large boats to transport cedar posts and wood from Promontory Point to Hooper. Presumably, it was one of those two boats that wrecked on the isle.

Four years after Nelson Arave's wreck on Fremont Island, one of his friends, Charles Smaltz, wrecked his large boat, too, on the island.

The *Salt Lake Tribune* of May 18, 1875, reported that the *City of Corrine* steamboat (150 feet long and three decks high) had carried eighty passengers on a recent Great Salt Lake excursion. However, a big storm struck, and at one point the fear was that the boat would capsize or sink. It didn't, but the boat was eventually anchored about two hundred yards offshore of Antelope Island to ride out the storm. This was "one of the roughest voyages ever experienced on the Salt Lake," according to the *Tribune* story.

The *Salt Lake Herald* of April 21, 1882, stated the dismal history of boating in the lake: "The fate of these steamers makes it clear that the people of Salt Lake City are not of a sea-going turn." The story also described the lake as "capacious."

Blanch Wenner, who lived on Fremont Island with her parents from 1886 to 1891, told the *Salt Lake Telegram* on June 17, 1939, that it sometimes took several days on a sailboat to reach the island in bad weather. At times, it required a stay on Antelope Island first.

The *Salt Lake Tribune* of September 21, 1913, mentions a lawsuit over the wreck of the boat *Argo*, which was used to transport sheep to Fremont Island and yet was destroyed in a storm on the lake in 1912.

Finally, fifteen Hooper boys took a thirty-four-foot boat to Fremont Island in 1924 and were stranded overnight when the boat's motor wouldn't start. They used signal fires to alert relatives but eventually got the motor running and returned to the mainland, according to the *Ogden Standard-Examiner* of February 24, 1924.

Even the 1930s weren't always safe on the lake. Hazel Cunningham of Salt Lake City had a goal of Great Salt Lake marathon swimming, and this effort highlighted the finicky lake's dangerous side. "Four Rescued as Boat Sinks in Lake Storm" was a June 1, 1936 headline in the *Salt Lake Telegram*.

Her first attempt at a record swim was met with disaster, as a sudden lake storm overturned the boat following along. A *Salt Lake Tribune* sportswriter and three of Cunningham's friends spent four hours in rough water with her before being rescued. The boat tipped over about three miles from Saltair Beach.

Just over a month later, Cunningham successfully made her record swim from Saltair to Antelope Island in fair weather.

There were, of course, shipwrecks on the lake after these. The bottom line is that the Great Salt Lake is not to be underestimated—even today.

SNAKE RIVER WATER
IN THE GSL?

The Great Salt Lake is declining. Between recent droughts and less river water reaching the lake, its level has sunk to all-time lows.

Ironically, in the early twentieth century, this possibility was not only recognized, but a solution was also offered. "Water for the Lake. Marcus E. Jones Has a Plan to Present. Would Use Snake River," was a December 27, 1903 headline in the *Salt Lake Tribune*.

Jones, a civil and mining engineer and geologist, proposed creating a canal that would bring the floodwaters from the Snake River and its tributaries to the Great Salt Lake and Utah. He said this would restore the GSL to its former normal levels and excess water from the canal could be used in other ways as needed. He estimated the cost for such a canal at $2 million (more than $50 million in 2022 value).

His plan was to take the water out of the Snake River at St. Anthony, Idaho, and take the canal through Red Rock Pass at the north end of the Cache Valley. There, the canal could dump into the Bear River, or a canal could shadow the river to the Wasatch Front. He said there is always excess Snake River water, especially during the months of April, May and June.

Jones's vision involved more than just raising the Great Salt Lake. His own studies concluded that the rainfall in the Salt Lake Valley is greater when the GSL is higher.

Of course, this canal never happened. Some two decades later, newspaper headlines were prophetic. "America's Famous 'Dead Sea' Soon to Be Dry Land," was a February 3, 1924 headline in the *Ogden Standard-Examiner*.

The Jackson Lake Dam, north of Jackson, Wyoming, controls the Snake River. The Snake was considered a new source of water in 1903 to raise the shrinking Great Salt Lake. *Author photo.*

"Within a century the Great Salt Lake, in Utah, will have dried up," the story stated. It then likened the GSL's reduction to that of its predecessor, Lake Bonneville.

The GSL fell ten feet from 1900 to 1915, until some exceptional wet years gained most of that loss back. "Were it to disappear, Salt Lake City would lose its principal attraction," the story stated.

Left would be an immense sink, a giant salty plain, impossible to use for anything constructive.

PART VI

KEY "WHAT IF?" SCENARIOS

I-15'S ALTERNATE ROUTE
IN DAVIS COUNTY

Imagine a mountain hugging Interstate 15 in north Davis County and southern Weber County. I-15 from Farmington to Ogden almost took a different route—Highway 89, instead of today's western route, near Highway 91.

The Ogden Chamber of Commerce pushed hard for the Highway 89 freeway option. After all, that offered the most direct access to Ogden City and then Weber State College. But an independent study revealed that it would be far more costly to build I-15 along the Highway 89 corridor. Also, the western route option offered more direct access to the military installations in northern Utah.

And once a Highway 89–aligned freeway reached Ogden, where would it go northward from there without impacting large sections of homes and businesses? According to Glen M. Leonard in his book *A History of Davis County*, the Federal Interstate Highway Act of 1956 expanded federal subsidies for major state highways. Washington paid 95 percent of the costs of such superhighways. It wasn't if freeways would be built in Utah but where.

Leonard's book states that increased traffic between Salt Lake City and Ogden is why the Utah State Road Commission chose a six-mile section in south Davis County to be Utah's first highway built to interstate standards. "In a ceremony in North Salt Lake in January 1958, Governor George D. Clyde launched the project by driving a bulldozer into Amasa Howard's ninety-year-old dairy barn to clear a route for the new $7.3-million segment,"

Highway 89 in Davis County follows the edge of the Wasatch Mountains. However, in the 1950s, one proposal had today's Interstate 15 located there. *Author photo.*

Leonard wrote. "Utah's first section of six-lane divided interstate highway reached north to Pages Lane and was completed in 1962."

Original plans did not include any interchanges between Farmington and Bountiful. Centerville had to lobby to eventually gain its own freeway access.

Bids for constructing I-15 in the Ogden area opened in 1963, split into several segments.

After three years of work, I-15 from south Layton to Ogden opened on November 23, 1966. A huge advantage with this section was that Main Street (Highway 91) would no longer be so congested with commuters during shift changes at Hill Air Force Base. The I-15 route north of Layton often followed the abandoned Bamberger Railroad route.

On December 12, 1976, the section of I-15 from the Box Elder–Weber County line to Perry was completed after more than four years of work. This meant that I-15 was now continuous from Layton to southern Box Elder County.

The section of the interstate from Lagoon to Layton was the last one finished in the Ogden area.

The widening and resurfacing of the existing section of Highway 91 from Layton to Lagoon was not open until 1977 through a $10 million project. Finally, uninterrupted freeway travel existed between Juab County on the south and Box Elder County on the north. Future projects would expand the freeway both north and south.

Leonard also noted that I-15 in Davis County produced a housing boom. "The communities along the freeway's route rightly envisioned a new incentive for growth," Leonard wrote. "Interstate 15 made the greatest difference in the Centerville, Farmington, and Kaysville areas, which had lagged behind other parts of the county because of their distance from both Ogden and Salt Lake City."

He continued: "Also, as in the Syracuse region, a stable agricultural population existed in the central core. Small subdivisions began appearing in these central cities about the time the interstate began reaching into the county from the south. Suburban sprawl brought the first, small subdivision to Syracuse in that same decade."

Utahns probably take I-15 for granted today, but intercity travel in northern Utah wasn't nearly as quick or convenient before the freeway came along.

WHEN OGDEN'S WATERFALL
WAS PURPOSELY MOVED

The treasured and historic waterfall in Ogden, Utah's Waterfall Canyon has always been exactly where it is now, right? Wrong. It was "moved" for about six months in the 1920s, though there is no mention of that feat in any history book.

The era wasn't called the Roaring Twenties for nothing. This was the time of national alcohol prohibition and, locally, when Weber County vainly tried to enforce a vast outdoor game preserve in the Wasatch Mountains from Weber Canyon to the North Ogden Divide. It was also when the Ogden Kiwanis Club, in cooperation with Ogden city officials, rerouted the waterfall itself in Waterfall Canyon for about six months, from November 1922 to May 1923.

Talk of rerouting the falls had surfaced more than a decade earlier. "Would Make Beautiful Falls," was a *Standard-Examiner* headline on June 1, 1912. H.C. Bigelow, president of the Ogden State Bank, said he would give the first $100 toward conveying the falls through a short flume farther to the northwest so that the falls could be visible from all points in the city. He believed this would be a 1,000 percent improvement in Ogden area scenery.

Arthur Kuhn, A.F. Parker, H.J. Craven and A.P. Bigelow were named later that month by the Ogden Publicity Bureau to a committee to study such a proposal, estimated to cost about $500. "City to Start Work on Falls, Cataract to Fall over Precipice in Full View of Ogden," read the *Standard* on September 20, 1922. "Queer Moving Job in Ogden Just Finished" was the headline on November 12 as the dream became a reality.

The one-hundred-foot falls at the end of Ogden's Waterfall Canyon. In the early 1920s, the waterfall was relocated west by piping so that it was more visible from the valley. That relocation lasted only a few months before vandals destroyed the piping system. *Taylor Arave photo.*

Why the project took more than a decade to come to fruition was never mentioned. "One of the strangest moving jobs ever undertaken in the west has just been completed-the removal of a waterfall," the story stated. No cost was mentioned. Pipes conveyed the water from "its old-tumbling over place" in the secluded southeast corner of Waterfall Canyon to a new spot, where "it now dashes over the rocks nearly 300 feet."

That presumably took the falls hundreds of feet to the northwest, where the vast cliffs below the south end of Malan's Peak made it much more visible from numerous vantage points and pretty much tripled its drop. (Otherwise, like today, the falls are visible only in the spring or in times of high water flow, ideally from the Thirtieth to the Thirty-Second Street area and best viewed from the west side of town.)

The water volume in November 1922 was noted as low, as usual, in the late fall season. Hopes of "a picturesque appearance" next spring and summer were dreamed of. But tragedy struck. "Vandals Ruin Unique Falls East of City, Project for Making Cataract Visible in Ogden Defeated," stated the May 13, 1923 *Standard*. "The result of many days of work and expenditures of hundreds of dollars have been wiped out through the malicious mischief of unknown persons in Waterfall Canyon."

A Boy Scouts executive made a trip up the canyon and found the pipeline utterly destroyed, with many joints hurled over cliffs. To repair the damage would cost almost as much as the original effort. Only a few sections of pipe were intact. "And now just when the falls would be most beautiful and a unique attraction the work has been undone by vandals," the *Standard* report concluded.

There's no more newspaper mention of repairing the damage; the project was simply abandoned and the falls reverted to their original course. But this vandalism was reminiscent of what happened in nearby Malan's Basin/ Heights, where vandals burned and destroyed what remained of the former hotel there, at around the same time.

Weber County was simply fascinated with waterfalls in the early twentieth century. There were numerous newspaper accounts of this appreciation of Waterfall Canyon. Another falls, the artificial waterfall (sometimes called "Rainbow Cataract" back then) at the mouth of Ogden Canyon, was also heralded and loved by residents. In fact, some newspaper stories confused or interchanged the two waterfalls.

42

WELCOME TO FREEDOM, UTAH

Here is another "what if?" proposition. Kaysville, Utah, was named for William Kay, first LDS Church bishop and pioneer settler in the area. However, the town was almost given a totally different name. The Kaysville Ward was organized in January 1851 by President Brigham Young, with Kay as bishop. The town was then known as "Kay's Settlement."

However, when Bishop Kay left the area, there was a desire by some settlers to change the community's name to Freedom. The *Deseret News* of November 21, 1860, even referred to the town by this name, so the alternate name did gain some traction and recognition.

The official name proposal was taken to President Young, who bluntly asked, "When did Kay's Ward get its freedom?" The idea was turned down, and Young strongly suggested the Kaysville name instead.

Freedom, Utah, does exist in the state today. It is a small, unincorporated agricultural community in Sanpete County four miles northwest of Manti. *Author photo.*

The Kaysville City Cemetery entrance. At one time in its early history, residents wanted to rename the town Freedom. *Author photo*.

Today, there is a Freedom town in Sanpete County, Utah, as well as one in western Wyoming.

43

BRYCE CANYON ALMOST HAD A LOOP ROAD

B ryce Canyon National Park had somewhat of a lackluster beginning, being in the shadows of the more highly esteemed sister park, Zion. Bryce has had some major "what ifs?": From almost altering its name and not using "Canyon" (since, geologically, it is not a canyon), to the site almost becoming only a Utah state park, to its being administratively under Zion Park until 1956.

Two more alternate histories can be added to that list. In 1931, there was a failed proposal to create a loop road from Highway 89 through Red Canyon to Bryce and then back to Highway 89 at Long Valley Junction. And in 1951, there was a strong move to build a road on the floor of Bryce Canyon itself.

"Government Plans New Road to Bryce Canyon," read the March 28, 1931 *Iron County Record* of Cedar City. This tentative loop road reached Rainbow Point (where the Bryce park highway ends southward today) and then would head due west to Highway 89 at the Long Valley Junction of U-14.

"The entire road would be about 27 miles long, with five miles being private lands and most of the balance in the Powell and Dixie national forests," the article stated. "The new road would make it possible to visit Bryce via the present route through Red Canyon and then return over an entirely different route, eliminating all retracing. Most of the route would be at 8,000-foot elevation and would add much to the pleasantness of the trip in hot summer months."

Hiking trails are the only way around the floor of Bryce Canyon National Park today. However, interior automobile roads were once proposed for the canyon bottom. *Author photo.*

Why didn't this road get built? Constructing the loop highway was contingent on Utah being able to cooperate and create five miles of road through the private lands. This apparently didn't happen, likely because of property acquisition issues. In addition, building the road to Long Valley Junction would have been a very costly path, with steep cliffs and eroding slopes.

Yes, the later proposal in 1951 was to build a paved road below the rim. "Civic Clubs Will Support Move for Road on Floor of Bryce Canyon," read an August 30, 1951 headline in the *Richfield Reaper.*

Bryce Canyon put Panguitch on the national map as the entrance, the last town before the now popular national park. The Associated Civics Clubs of Southern and Eastern Utah, along with the Panguitch Lions Club, held a meeting in town to discuss the idea of a road at the bottom of Bryce. "The Club agreed to support a suggestion by State Representative John Johnson of Tropic to the effect that a road can be built on the floor of Bryce Canyon so that visitors can view the real scenic attractions of the area," the Richfield newspaper stated. "The main beauty of Bryce Canyon cannot be seen from the rim of the canyon."

This view is looking southwest from near Bryce Canyon's Rainbow Point, where the paved road southward ends. However, a loop road was once proposed here to continue downward and westward to connect with Long Valley Junction and U.S. Highway 89. *Author photo*.

Of course, the inner road was never built, but it takes little imagination to envision a road going through the bottom of Bryce. Many natural features would have had to have been demolished to make room for such a road. Hiking would also not be the big activity it is today in Bryce with such a road. Why hike when you can drive down?

Here is some more history about Bryce Canyon National Park. In 1920, Bryce was just picking up steam with tourists. "Volunteers Repair Bryce Canyon Road," was a May 6 headline that year in the *Salt Lake Telegram*. A "road day club" had just been formed in Panguitch, with up to forty-seven men volunteering their time to smooth out the dirt road from Panguitch through Red Canyon and onto Bryce so that automobiles had better access.

Initially, for more than a decade, the road to Bryce Canyon ended at the northwest rim of the amphitheater, probably near today's Sunrise Point. Walking or horse travel was the only way farther south.

However, the *Salt Lake Tribune* of December 6, 1929, reported that the National Park Service had allocated $13,700 to survey and begin to construct a road eight or more miles long southward along the rim of Bryce in the

This is a May 18, 1956 photograph of an arch on Bryce Canyon National Park's Navajo Loop trail. Harold and Venice Flygare of Ogden, Utah (*left*), pose with two unidentified friends. The trail near here collapsed in the late 1990s, and the trail had to be rerouted. The collapse is perhaps another reason why a road at the bottom of Bryce Canyon might have been unsafe to build. *Author photo.*

summer of 1930. This road was "to afford visitors opportunity to view the canyon from many vantage points, instead of the one point now reached by the main highway," the *Tribune* story stated.

At the time, the National Park Service allocated $280,000 to improve roads along the North Rim of the Grand Canyon, particularly from the Bright Angel Camp to Point Imperial and Cape Royal.

Finally, while Zion has been host to many more accidents than Bryce, given its sheer cliffs and towering rocks, Bryce Canyon has also not been immune to accidents from falls. Three examples are provided here.

"Fall from Bryce Canyon Cliff Seriously Injures Cedar Girl," read the June 23, 1932 *Beaver County News*. The girl slipped off a cliff near Point Supreme and suffered three breaks in her pelvis bone and a broken arm. It took rescuers several hours to reach her.

"Girl Has Close Call in Utah Park Accident" stated the July 13, 1946 *Logan Herald-Journal*. The fourteen-year-old-girl from Buffalo, New York, slipped off a sandstone cliff in Bryce and went down one hundred feet "before she clutched the edge of a projecting chunk of sandstone, one of the many spires which have made the canyon famous." She was rescued with ropes by a park ranger. The girl's physician father treated her cuts and bruises, but nothing was broken.

The *Ogden Standard-Examiner* of April 22, 1954, reported that a sixty-one-year-old female tourist from Illinois died in a fall at the park on April 21. She stepped over a log barrier at the Far View Scenic Point, lost her balance and plunged ninety feet to her death down a cliff. She died instantly.

THE ALMOST SECOND GOLDEN SPIKE TALE

E ver hear the story about the second "Golden Spike"? It is just one of those intriguing things that was proposed and "might have been," but it didn't actually happen. It is also one of those fascinating historical footnotes, most of which are usually absent from the history books.

"Last Spike Will Be a Golden One," stated the November 21, 1903 *Ogden Standard-Examiner*. For the landmark completion of the wooden trestle shortcut across the Great Salt Lake, the Lucin Cutoff, big plans were proposed early.

The draft plan was that after driving the Golden Spike, it would be withdrawn and given to Union Pacific railroad baron E.H. (Edward) Harriman as a souvenir. In fact, it was speculated that Harriman himself might wield the sledge for the spike, at noon on Thanksgiving Day on the "Midlake" point of the trestle itself.

Being Thanksgiving, it was also suggested that a traditional holiday feast be prepared at one of the railroad camps along the Lucin Cutoff. But six days later, on November 27, at the actual event, "There was no golden spike driven," the *Standard* reported on that date.

Notwithstanding the lack of fanfare, the Lucin Cutoff was an engineering marvel for its day. It shaved 43.77 miles and 1,515 feet of climb off the original route to Promontory. Despite the completion observance on that Thanksgiving Day, the Lucin Cutoff didn't actually open to passenger trains and general traffic until almost ten months later, on September 16, 1904.

The construction of the Lucin Cutoff was said to feature a safety record superior to most other railroad projects, yet there were still some accidents.

The Golden Spike Historic Site, west of Brigham City, Utah, marking the completion of the transcontinental railroad in 1869. *Author photo.*

Replica locomotives at today's Golden Spike Historic Site. A second "golden spike" was almost driven in 1903, when the Lucin Cutoff was completed across the Great Salt Lake. *Author photo.*

The ceremony for the driving of the Golden Spike at Promontory Summit, Utah, on May 10, 1869, marking completion of the first transcontinental railroad. Samuel S. Montague (*center left*) of the Central Pacific Railroad shakes hands with Grenville M. Dodge of the Union Pacific Railroad (*center right*). *Photo by A.J. Russell, public domain.*

"Engine Overturns and Kills a Fireman," read the March 25, 1903 *Standard*. A portion of the trestle sinking was reported to have caused this accident at Lakeside, where Robert W. Watson was fatally crushed. Other Utah newspapers reported a "Quagmire without a bottom," as portions of the lakebed seemed bottomless.

It was in March 1903 that railroad builders battled what was almost a quicksand sinking in the Great Salt Lake. At one point in the building process, several hundred yards of earth were gulped down in the lake and caused a settling of some five feet.

Years later, after the Lucin Cutoff had been opened, "Severe Storm Injures Cut-Off," read the April 3, 1910 *Standard*. "Eighty-Mile Gale Lashes Waves to Fury and Damage Done," the subhead stated. Fortunately, on that particular day, strangely, no trains were scheduled to use the Lucin Cutoff. Still, the Southern Pacific reported that it had been strengthening the fill on the trestle for some time, anticipating possible damage such as this.

Technically, if a golden spike had been driven on the Lucin Cutoff, it would have been the second in Utah and at least the third golden spike used in the United States.

The Northern Pacific Railway did use a golden spike on September 8, 1883, to commemorate completion of a railroad track in Montana that served many nearby states. Former U.S. president Ulysses S. Grant drove in that final golden spike to mark the completion of a railroad line from the Great Lakes to the Pacific.

LOFTY MOUNTAIN ROADS NEVER BUILT

This is a tale of mountain roads dreamed of but never built.

Ogden-area residents were very excited about the advent of the automobile. In fact, they had dreams in the 1910s of constructing roads to the tops of prominent mountain peaks.

The first such dream appeared in the *Standard-Examiner* on June 25, 1912. "Why not build an automobile driveway to Lewis Peak or one of the other high mountains east of Ogden, so that even those not stout of heart and vigor of limb can reach the heights, see the grandeur of the mighty architectural work of Omnipotence and hitch wagons to the stars," the article stated.

That way, the story continued, even Postmaster Lewis Shurtliff, who was one of the first recorded to climb Lewis Peak, some sixty years earlier, could "go back in fancy to the days of long ago while a six-cylinder machine under low gear carried him up to the base of the peak in the clouds."

Ben Lomond Peak, almost a year later, was the next peak mentioned as needing an auto road. "From Ogden to a Peak above the Clouds" was the title of a May 20, 1913 story in the *Standard*. "To build and improve the road from Ogden to Ben Lomond peak by way of Liberty is a proposition that is receiving the support of a number of Ogden people, among whom is Attorney D.R. Roberts."

The report stated that the road would have to be made from the backside, from Liberty, as cliffs on the Ogden side prevent a road from there. "A road to that peak would attract autoists from all parts of the western country and no transcontinental tourist would pass by Ogden without making the visit to

Lewis Peak is one of the dominant mountains in the Ogden area. A road to its top was proposed in 1912 but never happened. *Author photo.*

the point," stated Roberts, who believed the road would be one of the most famous auto trips in America.

The report infers that there already was, in 1913, a road of sorts from Liberty (perhaps from today's North Fork Park area) partway to the back of Ben Lomond. Of course, neither the Lewis Peak nor the Ben Lomond road was ever built.

The two stories didn't mention the still existing "road" to Malan's Peak and Malan's Basin that went up Taylor Canyon, starting in 1892. This path was just wide enough for a horse and a special small wagon.

Salt Lakers were infected with the same conquering spirit. The *Davis County Clipper* reported on October 17, 1913, that the Salt Lake City Commission had ordered a survey made of a possible mountain road. This path would be made around the base of Ensign Peak and continue along the shoreline of Lake Bonneville to Mill Creek Canyon and eventually through the mountains to Morgan.

This report said city prisoners could do some of the construction, and big landowners along the route had already agreed to provide legal access. Some believed such a road would keep tourists in the Salt Lake area for days, weeks and months instead of just hours.

A road was proposed to the summit of Ben Lomond Peak, Ogden's most famous mountain, in 1913. It was never realized. *Author photo.*

Ensign Park, located straight north of downtown Salt Lake City. A road was proposed to its summit in 1913, but it was never realized. *Author photo.*

This road never happened, either, though today there is the "Scenic Backway" of Skyline Drive that goes from Farmington Canyon and along the mountaintop to Bountiful. But this dirt route lacks similar access to the Morgan side.

BIBLIOGRAPHY

Chapter 1

Arave, Lynn. "Name Repetition Confusion Abounds in Utah Outdoors." *Ogden (UT) Standard-Examiner*, July 13, 2015.

U.S. Geological Survey Database. "Utah Atlas & Gazetteer." DeLorme Mapping, 1993. https://ngmdb.usgs.gov.

Chapter 2

Arave, Lynn. "Utah's Biggest Fish Story." *Ogden Standard-Examiner*, May 20, 2015.

Box Elder News (Brigham City, UT). "New Highway Is Complete." September 9, 1924.

———. "Road to Be Free of Snow." October 14, 1924.

———. "A Studebaker Goes…." June 3, 1915.

Brainy Geography. www.brainygeography.com.

Jones, Brittny Goodsell. "Sardine Canyon: The Name's a Bit Fishy." *Logan (UT) Daily Herald*, October 12, 2008.

Logan (UT) Leader, September 24, 1880.

Rogers, Kristen. "Some Snow!! The Unforgettable Winter of 1948–49." Utah State History. http://history.utah.gov.

Sardine King.com. Email correspondence with author. www.sardineking.com, February 12, 2011.

U.S. Geological Survey. "Mount Pisgah, Utah" quadrangle map, revised 1996.

———. "Ogden, Utah" quadrangle map.

———. "Snow Basin, Utah" quadrangle map.

Utah State University Department of Ecology Center, Watershed Sciences. Email correspondence with author. October 6–7, 2011.

Utah State University Online Library. "View in Sardine Canyon, Utah, about 1910." www.digital.lib.usu.edu.

Van Cott, John W. *Utah Place Names*. Salt Lake City: University of Utah Press, 1990, 331.

Chapter 3

Arave, Lynn. "How About Dern Air Force Base Instead of Hill Air Force Base?" *Deseret News* (Salt Lake City, UT), September 19, 2020.

Davis County Clipper (Bountiful, UT). "Hill Air Force Base Celebrates Its Golden Anniversary." January 24, 1990.

Hill Top Times (Hill Air Force Base, UT). "Growth of Hill Field Reflected in Long List of Major Events." January 1, 1946.

Ogden Standard-Examiner. "Hard Working C of C., Davis Citizens Create Major Military Center." February 4, 1940.

Provo (UT) Daily Herald. "Hill Air Force Base Built on Strategic Site." November 18, 1999.

Chapter 4

Arave, Lynn. "St. George Likely Named after an LDS Apostle." *Deseret News*, July 8, 2007.

Jenson, Andrew. "Encyclopedia History of The Church of Jesus Christ of Latter-day Saints." *Deseret (UT) Press*, 1941.

Leigh, Rufos Wood. *Five Hundred Utah Place Names*. Salt Lake City: University of Utah Press, 1961.

Powell, Allan Kent. "St. George." *Utah History Encyclopedia*. Salt Lake City: University of Utah Press, 1994.

St. George, Utah. www.sgcity.org.

Van Cott, John W. *Utah Place Names*. Salt Lake City: University of Utah Press, 1990.

CHAPTER 5

Arave, Lynn. "What's in a Name? A Slew of Western History." *Deseret News*, July 27, 2009.

Burton, Doris Karren. "A History of Uintah County." Utah State Historical Society, 1996.

O'Neil, Floyd, director emeritus of the American West Center. Telephone interview with author. July 2009.

Powell, Allan Kent. State of Utah historian. Telephone interview with author. July 10, 2009.

Van Cott, John W. *Utah Place Names*. Salt Lake City: University of Utah Press, 1990.

CHAPTER 6

Davis County Clipper. "Layton Lines." May 29, 1896.

Layton City, Utah. www.laytoncity.org.

Utah State History. www.history.utah.gov.

Weekly Reflex (Kaysville, UT). "David E. Layton, Davis's Oldest Recalls Layton's Early History." October 24, 1957.

CHAPTER 7

Arave, Lynn. "When a New Name Was Sought for Bryce Canyon. Plus, the Scoop on Nearby Ruby's Inn." *Deseret News*, May 13, 2019.

BIBLIOGRAPHY

Salt Lake Herald. "New Name Wanted for Bryce Canyon." June 8, 1920.
Sherman, John Dickinson. "Zion: Rival of Yosemite." *Ephraim (UT) Enterprise*, November 29, 1919.

CHAPTER 8

Arave, Lynn. "The Scoop on 'Watkins Dam.'" *Ogden Standard-Examiner*, May 15, 2014.
Weber Basin Water Conservancy District. "History." www.weberbasin.com.
Willard Bay Reservoir. U.S. Bureau of Reclamation. www.usbr.gov.

CHAPTER 9

Arave, Lynn. "Major Ogden Streets Have Presidential Ring." *Deseret News*, December 10, 2007.
Ogden Standard-Examiner. "The Streets Have Been Renamed by the City Council." April 6, 1889.
Roberts, Richard C., and Richard W. Sadler. *A History of Weber County*. Salt Lake City: Utah State Historical Society, 1997.

CHAPTER 10

Arave, Lynn. "North Ogden No Longer Stumped for Frogwater." *Deseret News*, June 1, 2000.
Bicentennial Park. North Ogden City. www.northogdencity.com.
Hislop, Charles C. Telephone interview with author. November 1999.
Historic plaques. Bicentennial Park, North Ogden, Utah.

CHAPTER 11

Arave, Lynn. "Quirky Utah Place Names." *Deseret News*, December 25, 2000.

Delicate Arch. National Park Service. www.nps.gov.

Times-Independent (Moab, UT). "Move to Make National Park of Arches Monument." March 29, 1934.

Van Cott, John W. *Utah Place Names.* Salt Lake City: University of Utah Press, 1990.

Chapter 12

Arave, Lynn. "Bigfoot: A Search in Utah." *Deseret News*, June 24, 2009.

———. "Tracking Bigfoot: Real or Not, the Creature Haunts Us." *Deseret News*, April 1, 1993.

———. "Utah Man Says He's Seen Bigfoot 9 Times Since '68." *Deseret News*, June 7, 1997.

Daily Spectrum (St. George, UT). "Bigfoot Seen Again." February 29, 1980.

Logan Daily Herald. "Hiker Thinks He Saw Bigfoot." August 31, 1977.

Ogden Standard-Examiner. "Seen Bigfoot?" August 27, 1977.

Provo Daily Herald. "2 Utahns Say They Sighted Bigfoot." February 13, 1980.

Utah Bigfoot Research. Interview with Ray Layton. March 20, 1990.

Chapter 13

Arave, Lynn. "Legend of the Bear Lake Monsters—Yes, in the Plural." *Deseret News*, October 10, 2017.

———. "Mythical Beasts Lurk in 5 Utah Lakes." *Deseret News*, September 23, 2001.

Corrine (UT) Reporter. "The Bear Lake Monster." May 20, 1871.

Deseret Evening News. "Monster Story." August 20, 1868.

Deseret News. "Editorial Correspondence." June 30, 1869.

———."Mammoth." October 14, 1868.

Logan Herald Republican. "Quil Nebeker Sees Monster. Verifies Mooney and Horne's Story of the Bear Lake Terrorizer and Gives Own Experience." September 21, 1907.

Logan Republican. "Bear Lake Monster Appears." September 18, 1907.

Ogden Standard-Examiner. "Lake Monsters, Flying Serpents, Hairy Creatures." May 30, 2014.

Utah State University Digital Collections. "Bear Lake Monster." www. digital.lib.usu.edu.

CHAPTER 14

Arave, Lynn. "Great Tales Surrounding the Great Salt Lake; Its Briny Bowels Are Filled with Monster Myths." *Deseret News*, August 1, 1999.
Deseret News. "Quite Fishy." July 18, 1877.
Salt Lake Herald, July 13, 1877.
Salt Lake Telegram. "Great Horned Monster with Lizard's Body, Leaps Like a Giant Kangaroo." April 30, 1902.

CHAPTER 15

Arave, Lynn. "Canadian in Utah to Seek 'Strange Creatures Seldom Seen'." *Deseret News*, December 27, 2009.
———. "Lake Monsters, Flying Serpents, Hairy Creatures." *Ogden Standard-Examiner*, May 30, 2014.
Deseret News. "Monster Snake." December 25, 1873.
Ogden Standard-Examiner. "A Veritable Eden. The Serpent Is at His Old Tricks Again." July 23, 1894.
Salt Lake Telegram. "'Gorilla' Man Attacks Woman on S.L. Street." December 18, 1931.
———. "Great Horned Monster with Lizard's Body, Leaps like a Giant Kangaroo." April 30, 1902.

CHAPTER 16

Arave, Lynn. "Colorful Tales Abound in Red-Rock Country." *Deseret News*, July 24, 2000.
Arave, Lynn, and Jody Genessy. "Living in Utah: A Guide to Separate Reality from Myths." *Deseret News*, July 24, 2003.

Lee, Hector. "The Three Nephites: The Substance and Significance of the Legend in Folklore." PhD dissertation. University of New Mexico, 1947.

Pratt, Orson. "Gathering of Israel." *Journal of Discourses*. Vol. 18: 26.

———. "Progress of the Work." *Journal of Discourses*. Vol. 2, 264, April 7, 1855.

CHAPTER 17

Arave, Lynn. "Colorful Tales Abound in Red-Rock Country." *Deseret News*, July 24, 2000.

———. "'Resurrecting' Utah's Biggest April Fools' Hoaxes." *Deseret News*, March 31, 2000.

Book of Mormon Helaman 6:18–29.

Daily Spectrum. "Folktales' Mischief Blamed on 'Gadianton Robbers.'" February 17, 1996.

Deseret News, December 28, 1854.

Young, Brigham. *Journal of Discourses*. Vol. 8, 344, January 20, 1861.

CHAPTER 18

Arave, Lynn. "Myth Grew about Lack of Trees in Salt Lake." *Deseret News*, July 24, 2004.

Historical marker. 600 East Street between 300–400 South Street, Salt Lake City.

Jackson, Richard, professor of geography at Brigham Young University. Telephone interview with author. July 2004.

Salt Lake Telegram. "Lone Cedar Tree to Be Fenced." August 13, 1924.

Utah Historical Markers. "Lone Cedar Tree." www.utahhistoricalmarkers.org.

CHAPTER 19

Arave, Lynn. "In 1902, Utah's 2 Oldest Pioneers Had Visited Utah First in 1846." *Deseret News*, July 22, 2019.

———. "Looking Back on the Good—and Bad—First Impressions Pioneers Had of the Salt Lake Valley." *Deseret News*, July 21, 2018.

Deseret Evening News. "Brother and Sister Who Came to Utah in 1846." July 23, 1904.

———. "Utah Legends, Indians, Trappers and Pioneers." December 15, 1906.

Deseret News. "The State's Lost Gold Mine." July 22, 2019.

Kimball, Solomon F. "Early-Day Recollections of Antelope Island." *Improvement Era Magazine* 10, no. 5 (March 1907): 334–39.

Chapter 20

Arave, Lynn. "Looking Back on the Good—and Bad—First Impressions Pioneers Had of the Salt Lake Valley." *Deseret News*, July 21, 2018.

Hunter, Milton R. *Utah in Her Western Setting*. Salt Lake City, UT: Sun Lithographing, 1956.

Chapter 21

Arave, Lynn. "Mormon Battalion Gold 'Purchased' Ogden Area." *Ogden Standard-Examiner*, December 5, 2013.

Daughters of Utah Pioneers, Weber County Chapter. *Beneath Ben Lomond's Peak: A History of Weber County 1824–1900*. Salt Lake City, UT: Quality Press, 1995

Hunter, Milton R. *The Utah Story*. Salt Lake City, UT: Wheelwright Lithographing Company, 1960.

National Mining Association. www.nma.org.

Ogden City, Utah. www.ogdencity.com.

Terry, William W. *Weber County Is Worth Knowing*. N.p.: Self-published, 1987.

CHAPTER 22

Arave, Lynn. "Pioneer Trek: Historical Sites around State Give a Glimpse into Utah's Heritage." *Deseret News*, July 23, 2015.
———. "Some Myths Accompany Stories of Pioneers' Arrival." *Deseret News*, July 24, 2008.
Kimball, Stanley B., PhD. "Mormon Pioneer: Historic Resource Study." Washington, DC: National Park Service, 1991.
LeBaron, Benjamin. "The Grasshopper War" (typescript). Hurricane, Utah, April 9, 1939.

CHAPTER 23

Adams, Elias Harris. *Elias Adams: A Pioneer Profile*. Adams, UT: self-published, 2007.
Grayson, Don. "Holocene Bison in the Great Basin, Western USA." *Holocene* (September 1, 2006). journals.sagepub.com.
Lupo, Karen D. "The Historical Occurrence and Demise of Bison in Northern Utah." *Utah Historical Quarterly* 64, no. 2 (1996).
Russell, Osborne. Russell kept a detailed journal of his nine years (1834–43) in the Rocky Mountains.

CHAPTER 24

Arave, Lynn. "April Fool! Fake Volcanoes and Frankenstein Are among Utah's Classic Pranks and Hoaxes." *Deseret News*, March 30, 2018.
Salt Lake Telegram, November 2, 1902.
———, November 18, 1902.
Salt Lake Tribune, March 8, 1897.

CHAPTER 25

Ancestry.com.

Arave, Lynn. "April Fool! Fake Volcanoes and Frankenstein Are among Utah's Classic Pranks and Hoaxes." *Deseret News*, March 30, 2018.

Newton Town Library. The library provides a detailed account of the prank. 51 South Center Street, Newton, Utah, 84327-0578.

CHAPTER 26

Arave, Lynn. "South Weber, Hooper Forever Changed by Ecclesiastical Dispute." *Ogden Standard-Examiner*, November 21, 2013.

Bell, Lee D. *South Weber: The Autobiography of One Utah Community*. N.p.: unknown publisher, 1990.

Carr, Annie Call. *East of Antelope Island*. Salt Lake City, UT: Daughters of Utah Pioneers, Davis County Chapter. 3rd ed., 1969.

Deseret News, March 8, 1855.

Leonard, Glen M. *A History of Davis County* (Utah Centennial County History Series). Farmington, UT: Davis County Commission, 1999.

CHAPTER 27

Arave, Lynn. "Women Started the First Collegiate Basketball in Utah and Even Beat the Men." *Deseret News*, February 21, 2018.

Deseret News, January 19, 1900.

Ludlow, Daniel H. *Encyclopedia of Mormonism*. Vol. 3. Provo, UT: Brigham Young University, 1992, pp. 877–78.

Salt Lake Herald, May 17, 1897.

Salt Lake Tribune. "Basket-Ball Maidens. The Elusive Sphere Chased Behind Closed Doors." November 6, 1897.

———. "University Basket-Ball. Girls Defeat the Boys in the First Open Game." May 16, 1897.

———, April 18, 1897.

———, June 4, 1897.

CHAPTER 28

Arave, Lynn. "Back when Football Was Deemed Too Dangerous to Play at BYU—and Almost in the Entire State." *Deseret News*, November 21, 2017.
Deseret News, December 8, 1905.
Ogden Standard-Examiner. "Football Contest." November 24, 1885.
Salt Lake Tribune. "Mormon Church Is against Football." November 18, 1908.
———. "Present Football Is Too Dangerous." November 19, 1909.

CHAPTER 29

Arave, Lynn. "Baseball Broke In on 1930 Conference Talk." *Deseret News*, September 26, 1998.
Dehnel, John, KSL Radio head engineer. Telephone interview with author. September 1998.
Elder David B. Haight's office, The Church of Jesus Christ of Latter-day Saints. Telephone interview with author. September 1998.

CHAPTER 30

Arave, Lynn. "When Sir Edmund Hillary of Mount Everest Fame Hiked the High Uintas—Twice, and More Mountain Tales." *Deseret News*, September 22, 2018.
Deseret News. "Famed Climber Cites Uinta's 'Smiling' Peaks." July 11, 1962.
Uinta Basin Standard (Roosevelt, UT). "New Zealand Mountain Climber and Family Thrilled with Pack Trip into High Uintas Areas." July 19, 1962.

CHAPTER 31

Brigham Young University. Scholars Archive. www.scholarsarchive.byu.edu.
Church of Jesus Christ Temples. www.ldschurchtemples.com.
Ensign. "The Manti Temple" (March 1978).
LDS Church News (March 8, 1958).

Stubbs, Glen R. *A Temple on the Hill: A History of the Manti Temple*. Rexburg, ID: Ricks College Press, 1976.

Utah Pioneer Stories. Sanpete County. www.sanpete.com.

CHAPTER 32

Ogden Standard-Examiner. "Gold Exposed by Bolt of Lightning." June 26, 1913.

———, August 31, 1904.

———, October 6, 1899.

Salt Lake Tribune. "Ogden's Lost Mine Taylor Canyon Holds the Secret of a Mine Abandoned Nearly 50 Years." October 18, 1959.

CHAPTER 33

American Fork Citizen. July 13, 1978.

Box Elder News, April 19, 1906.

Davis County Clipper. "Dancing Master Proves to Be Spy. Man Who Taught Dancing at The Lagoon Tried to Blow Up Pavilion on Soldiers' Day." September 7, 1917.

———. "Earl E. Logston Killed after Races." September 9, 1921.

———. "Emma Youngquist Drowned at Lagoon." August 2, 1912.

———. "Ogden Man Killed on Dipper at Lagoon." August 1, 1924.

———. "Park City Miner Meets Death at Lagoon July 4." July 10, 1925.

———. "Park City Woman Accidentally Killed at Lagoon." July 18, 1930.

———, June 5, 1908.

———, August 28, 1908.

Deseret Evening News, August 5, 1907.

Deseret News, April 23, 1907.

———, May 1, 1989.

———, June 11, 1989.

———, June 12, 1989.

———, August 1, 2004.

———, September 9, 1954.

Lakeside Review. "Guard OK after Attack by Caribou at Lagoon." September 11, 1980.

Logan Journal. "Jimmie Johns Is Shot by Officers." July 18, 1960.

Ogden Standard-Examiner. "Auto Racer at Lagoon Killed." July 25, 1922.

———. "Fall at Lagoon Hurts Employee." May 31, 1976.

———. "Gay Lagoon Coaster Ride Injures Eight." July 30, 1954

———. "Railroad Man Is Killed at Lagoon." July 16, 1914.

———. "Thugs Bind Guard, Get Lagoon Cash." June 5, 1950.

———, July 29, 1912.

Provo Daily Herald. "Bad Wire Shocks Lagoon Visitors, One Employee." June 20, 1989.

———, May 20, 1996.

———, June 21, 1983.

Salt Lake Herald. "Sixteen-Year-Old Boy Arrested for Trying to Wreck Lagoon Train." August 26, 1903.

———, June 20, 1900.

———, July 6, 1896.

Salt Lake Herald Journal, July 7, 1975.

Salt Lake Herald Republican. "Accident at Lagoon. Reckless Man Causes Injury to Several Children." July 19, 1902.

Salt Lake Telegram. "Four Arrested for Burglary." November 20, 1934.

———. "Train Victim, 5, 'Poor' in Hospital." August 31, 1951.

———, August 5, 1952.

———, August 18, 1942.

———, August 21, 1934.

———, September 2, 1946.

Salt Lake Tribune. "Davis Nabs Two Juveniles on Wounding of Woman." May 22, 1951.

———. "Husband Dies after Saving Wife in Flood." August 14, 1923.

———. "Lagoon Worker Hurt in Fracas." July 17, 1959.

———. "Ride at Lagoon Hurts Worker." June 28, 1964.

———. "Shooting at Lagoon. Bartender Alexander Has Encounter with Thieves. They Wanted Free Beer." June 17, 1897.

———. "Shots Fail to Stop Youths After Lagoon Car Crash." August 28, 1951.

———. "2 Salt Lakers Jailed after Shooting." August 3, 1961.

———, April 21, 1968.

———, August 2, 1961.

Weekly Reflex. "Man Arrested for Beating Up Girl at Lagoon May 30." June 5, 1930.

————. "M.L. Rose Seriously Injured at Lagoon." July 8, 1915.

————. "Rocking Boat Brings Death to Young Boy." June 30, 1927.

————. "Three Injured When Lagoon Balloon Bursts." August 21, 1924.

————, July 17, 1930.

————, August 20, 1942.

CHAPTER 34

Arave, Lynn. "Land of the Lake: What's In, Under and Around the Great Salt Lake?" *Deseret News,* June 12, 1994.

Currey, Don, University of Utah geography professor. Telephone interview with author. *Deseret News*, April 1995.

Phillips, Steve, media coordinator for the Utah Division of Wildlife Resources. Telephone interview with author. *Deseret News*, April 1995.

Wallace Gwynn, saline geologist with the Utah Geological Survey. Telephone interview with author. *Deseret News*, April 1995.

CHAPTER 35

Arave, Lynn. "From a 'Lakemobile' to a Stroll to Fremont Island." *Ogden Standard-Examiner*, October 23, 2014.

Miller, David E. "Saltwater Trail on the Desert" *Desert Magazine* 12, no. 7 (May 1949), 4–8.

CHAPTER 36

Diesel Brothers. "Great Salt Lake Eats Tractors, Vehicles, and People!" YouTube. October 18, 2020. www.youtube.com.

Ogden Standard-Examiner. "Horses Die in Quicksand of Great Salt Lake after Driver Missed Stakes Marking Route. Ogdenite Is Haunted by Experience as Steeds Drown." May 28, 1939.

————. "Hunters Again Foiled in Phantom Coyote Chase. New Expedition Scheduled." March 31, 1944.
————. "Phantom Coyote Has Hunters Marooned in Lake." March 29, 1944.
————. "Phantom of Isle Still Eludes Dogs." March 26, 1944.
————. "New Speculation Arises about Island Cross." November 2, 1943.
Salt Lake Herald Republican. "Has Another Sinking Spell." March 19, 1903.
Salt Lake Tribune. "Island Coyote Killed in Lake Waters." April 4, 1944.

Chapter 37

Arave, Lynn. "Is Antelope Island Misnamed? Back When Transplanted Antelope Refused to Stay There." *Deseret News,* December 16, 2020.
Davis County Clipper, September 12, 1924.
————, November 17, 1933.
Hancock, Harvey. "Island Offers Nature Study. Antelopes Refused to Remain. Bathing Beaches Unsurpassed." *Salt Lake Telegram,* July 2, 1922.
Salt Lake Tribune. "To Island by Land. Trip Can Be Made Practically Dry Shod. Road of Salt and Sand." September 24, 1900.

Chapter 38

Arave, Lynn. "Early Shipwrecks on the Briny and Unpredictable Great Salt Lake." *Deseret News,* April 8, 2020.
Ogden Standard-Examiner, February 24, 1924.
Salt Lake Herald, April 21, 1882.
Salt Lake Tribune, May 2, 1872.
————, May 18, 1875.
————, September 21, 1913.
Salt Lake Telegram. "Four Rescued as Boat Sinks in Lake Storm." June 1, 1936.
————, June 17, 1939.

CHAPTER 39

Arave, Lynn. "When the Snake River Was Proposed as the Shrinking Great Salt Lake's Lasting Salvation." *Deseret News*, August 13, 2019.

Ogden Standard-Examiner. "America's Famous 'Dead Sea' Soon to Be Dry Land." February 3, 1924.

Salt Lake Tribune. "Water for the Lake. Marcus E. Jones Has a Plan to Present. Would Use Snake River." December 27, 1903.

CHAPTER 40

Arave, Lynn. "I-15 Almost Followed US 89 Near Mountains." *Ogden Standard-Examiner*, April 23, 2015.

Leonard, Glen M. *A History of Davis County* (Utah Centennial County History Series) Davis County Commission, 1999.

CHAPTER 41

Arave, Lynn. "When Ogden Relocated Its Treasured Waterfall." *Ogden Standard-Examiner*, April 11, 2014.

Ogden Standard-Examiner. "City to Start Work on Falls, Cataract to Fall Over Precipice in Full View of Ogden." September 20, 1922.

———. "Queer Moving Job in Ogden Just Finished." November 12, 1922.

———. "Would Make Beautiful Falls." June 1, 1912.

CHAPTER 42

Deseret News. "Excursion through the Northern Counties." June 20, 1860.

———. November 21, 1860.

Van Cott, John W. *Utah Place Names*. Salt Lake City: University of Utah Press, 1992.

CHAPTER 43

Arave, Lynn. "A Pair of Never Built Roads in Bryce Canyon National Park." *Deseret News*, June 24, 2020.

Beaver County News. "Fall from Bryce Canyon Cliff Seriously Injures Cedar Girl." June 23, 1932.

Iron County Record (Cedar City, UT). "Government Plans New Road to Bryce Canyon." March 28, 1931.

Logan (UT) Herald-Journal. "Girl Has Close Call in Utah Park Accident." July 13, 1946.

Ogden Standard-Examiner, April 22, 1954.

Richfield (UT) Reaper. "Civic Clubs Will Support Move for Road on Floor of Bryce Canyon." August 30, 1951.

Salt Lake Telegram. "Volunteers Repair Bryce Canyon Road." May 6, 1920.

Salt Lake Tribune, December 6, 1929.

CHAPTER 44

Arave, Lynn. "The Tale of the Second Golden Spike." *Ogden Standard-Examiner*, February 19, 2015.

Ogden Standard-Examiner. "Engine Overturns and Kills a Fireman." March 25, 1903.

———. "Last Spike Will Be a Golden One." November 21, 1903.

———. "Severe Storm Injures Cut-Off." April 3, 1910.

———. "There Was No Golden Spike Driven…." November 27, 1903.

CHAPTER 45

Arave, Lynn. "Dreams of Lofty Roads Never Built." *Ogden Standard-Examiner*, May 23, 2014.

Davis County Clipper, October 17, 1913.

Ogden Standard-Examiner. "From Ogden to a Peak Above the Clouds." May 20, 1913.

———, June 25, 1912.

ABOUT THE AUTHOR

Lynn Arave graduated from Weber State University with degrees in communications-journalism and human performance. He worked for the *Deseret News* for thirty-two years, first as a sportswriter, then as a feature writer and finally as a city desk reporter and editor. He has written many other books, including *Walking Salt Lake City;* Images of America: *Layton, Utah*; *Detour Utah: Mysteries, Legends and Peculiar Places.* He also maintains many Google blogs, including *The Mystery of Utah History*. Lynn lives in Layton with his wife, LeAnn Flygare Arave. The couple has four children: Roger, Steven, Elizabeth and Taylor; plus, four grandchildren.